LET IT FLOW

BRIAN O. MOHIKA

ACKNOWLEDGEMENTS

This book is dedicated to anyone who ever quit on their dreams.

Consider this a wake up call to dream again, and this time . . . don't quit!

- Edwin Alvarez, thank you for helping me grow into a business owner. We made the "foxhole" work, didn't we?

- Miguel Lopez, thank you for being the eyes of the journey when we needed you! You're up next!

- To my high school English teacher, who told me I would never graduate college or be anything significant in life. At the time, you were right. You motivated me beyond measure.

- Oriana Beaudet, DNP, RN, PHN, thank you for inviting me to the American Nurses Association Innovation Advisory Board. I now can reach more nurses and inspire them not to quit on their ideas and advance the nursing profession.

- General Earl Les Brinkley, thank you for giving me the title for the book in 2019. I thought you were kidding when you told me I was going to write a second book. I look forward to reading your (almost released) book, "Spiritual General."

- Lastly, to my best friend, life partner, and wonderful wife, Eunice. I can't thank you enough for designing this book cover and helping me never to hit the snooze button. I love you!

TABLE OF CONTENTS

FOREWORD

A Criminal Justice and English major who pivoted to Nursing and somehow ended up as the founder of a digital marketing agency. That's my path. Nursing takes you on many paths and leads you to incredible journeys of compassion and innovation.

The days of nurses only working at the bedside or as a disposable, replaceable employee are over. Nurses realize their value. We're choosing the lives we want. We understand that we have so much to offer in healthcare and use our nursing skills, education, and experience to carve out our paths.

Entrepreneurship and innovation are worlds of pivoting, cultivating, creating, and shaping lives. Yes, it's hard work. It's you looking back at your mistakes, bloopers, and failed business ventures with gut-wrenching laughs. It is a pain, pleasure, and even comedy at times. It is fun and hard work simultaneously. Often, it's you reinventing yourself and starting something new.

Brian came from a similar path. He is a nurse who saw a problem and created a solution. He chose to follow his path. He took his nursing knowledge and passion for helping people and took a chance . . . without knowing the outcome.

His idea could have tanked. And who knows where he'll be in ten years. But he chose to be bold. He decided not to wait.

Now is not the moment to wait. Now is not the time to sit on the sidelines. It's not the time to doubt yourself, your visions, or your dreams. It's time for you to be bold, to create your path. Now is the time to choose the life you love and to get those ideas out of your head. Now is the time, as Brian appropriately titled this book, to "Let It Flow."

PORTIA WOFFORD

PREFACE

Nurse entrepreneurship. Nurse innovation. If one would Google these two phrases, that person would find pages upon pages of results. Head to Amazon or Barnes and Noble, and you are likely to see an entire section on innovation and entrepreneurship. So why another book on these topics?

I cannot recall a time during grade school or high school where my teachers expressed I could become an entrepreneur or even an inventor, for that matter. I had always been taught to grow up and be a productive employee and someday even become a manager of some sort. When I began my medical career, I still never thought of owning my business, nor did anyone ever take the time to teach me this either. I envisioned myself working in a hospital setting for the length of my career because that is what I saw everyone else doing. I wanted to write this book to help break those professional chains which can weigh us down and hinder our progress from impacting healthcare and improving a person's quality of life. I firmly believe the more transparent we are in life, the easier it is to help people grow through our stories, whether good or bad. I decided to share intimate details of my entrepreneurial journey to inspire others to break free from any paradigms that may have been set by those who have come before us. My goal is to encourage the reader of this book to believe in their inventions and innovations and remove any fear and doubt of the possibility of becoming a successful entrepreneur yourself.

When I began searching and reading books on innovation, I found them to be very systematic. Sure, you have a step-by-step guide on what to do, but the one thing I've learned as a nurse is the importance of connection. We need connections. Sometimes it is the difference between saving a patient and losing one. I want to share my failures and testimonies along with the professional journey to connect. When you talk to people about your success stories, people will listen and be inspired, but most will not understand because of not experiencing the same results within their ventures. Unfortunately, most people identify with other people through failures because the truth is, there are not enough success stories to grasp this reality. I want you to not only listen, learn, and be inspired, but I would like for you to connect with my story. I want you to understand the struggles, the battles, the wins, the losses. I want you to see yourself in my story. Have you noticed that when you speak about your pitfalls or mistakes, people will readily identify with you and say things like, "Oh yeah," or "Oh my God, I did too! I went through the same thing!" Once we connect on this intimate level, you'll understand how and why I overcame and fought for every dream and goal I now have. You will see that it is obtainable. Reaching people who desire to become innovators and inventors themselves is the goal of this book. I want to connect with people to help them grow and advance patient care by connecting with the readers on all professional path levels.

No one can implement quality patient care the way a nurse does—LPN and RN alike. We need to stop looking at nurses by a title. We need to stop asserting leadership on someone just because they have a Ph.D. Just because one may have a Ph.D. does not mean that that person is a leader. It just means he/she has a Ph.D. In no way would I attempt to mitigate academia of any level. I want to emphasize the heart of leadership, courage, inspiration, change, teamwork, innovation, and people; if people can't work with you, your degree is nothing but a plaque on the wall. It's not about personal accomplishments. It's not about the title. It's about the heart. These qualities are the reasons why nurses are at the forefront because we give our hearts. We offer our all. Inventions and innovations are the byproducts of providing excellent patient care. If you provide excellent patient care, then you will be able to see things that other people won't because of your passion for loving people; whether you're an LPN, an RN, or even if you have a Ph.D. or DNP, you'll make a difference. What makes you a nurse is your ability to completely lay down your life for a patient and go above and beyond helping this patient. And that is why it can be so dangerous for a nurse to navigate in the business realm. This type of thought process is not how to open a business; laying down and giving it your heart with this emotional push, which we'll touch on later in this book, will not get you a successful business. This book will show you the need to balance your nursing (or healthcare) emotions to navigate the entrepreneurial world.

These are the reasons why I wanted to start with my heart and my feelings. I wanted to share what I've learned in opening a business and what I've learned about removing my emotions. I've learned many valuable lessons along this journey, which has also transcended into other areas of my life and helped me grow as a person.

INTRODUCTION

Nurses have always been innovative. Finding ways to improve care is second nature to almost every nurse. It is not something we think about it. It is something we do practically impulsively. Nurses are responsible for some of the most transformative inventions used in healthcare:

- Sister Jean Ward: Neonatal Phototherapy

- Anita Dorr: The crash cart

- Teri Barton-Salina and Gail Barton-Hay: Color-coded IV Lines

- Adda May Allen: Baby bottles with disposable liners

- Bessie Bount-Griffin: Feeding tube for paralyzed veterans

- Elise Sorensen: Ostomy bags

- Ernesto Holguin: Diabetic foot ulcer prevention

The list goes on and on.

But, when nurses reach out to me to invent something, there seems to be a few common problems.

1. They have an idea and haven't pushed forward with it.

2. They have an idea but don't want to give up any control or equity in the company to keep the momentum of growth.

3. The decisions they have made aren't pushing their ideas forward.

Do you know what the problem with this is? Patients and healthcare suffer when your ideas are not developed. If nurses are not on the frontlines of innovation, healthcare suffers. What if you don't fail? Think of all the people you're going to impact. We seem to have built obstacles in our mind which only hinders the growth of patient care. Life has accustomed many to think of what can go wrong when we are beginning a new journey. It is critical to understand the beginning of anything is a delicate time in itself. Embrace the moment. Live in the suspense of the unknown, and greatness will navigate you through life. In turn, inventions and innovations Life is better lived walking with a blind faith with clinical experience as the flashlight illuminating your path on each step. An invention is something tangible, and innovation is changing or enhancing a system that increases in value. I may use these terms (invention and innovation) interchangeably as we get to the larger picture of improving patient care because, to me, they are so closely tied together. Whether it is invention or innovation, there is always a high risk of any project within a healthcare setting. There are so many times in a human's life where we take unnecessary risks, and why not take one more to impact healthcare and improve the patient's quality of life? Nurses are the number one trusted profession within the last 20 years. Healthcare workers are always trusted to keep the patient safe and never do any harm.

I never knew I could become an entrepreneur when I entered healthcare, particularly in nursing school. I always envision myself being at the bedside, essentially for my entire career. I know enough about myself to know that I didn't want to have any executive positions outside of the clinical setting. I never even realized a completely different career field where one can still be a nurse and still be his/her own boss. We never had a nursing school class that would teach us any business basics or the process of inventing a medical device or improving innovation. In my personal life, I never had somebody explain to me the gift of turning rejection into the ultimate motivator, which will fuel your entrepreneurial skills and ambitions. We do have to be mindful of knowing the difference between rejection and our expectations. We have felt rejected, but in reality, it was that somebody did not meet our expectations. Expectations are an accountability issue within ourselves, and we must keep expectations low with hope for the best in every scenario--in life and the business world. Being in business is like being in a war. The emotionally rejected will never survive. The corrected expectations will walk you right into your promise and successes in life. Once I lowered my expectations of people, projects, leads, goals, and outcomes in general, I was able to get the best out of life. Rejection and expectations are a balance, and being able to master this balance will determine where your project ends up after all is said and done.

Before we dive into the meat and potatoes, let's discuss breakfast.

Money.

I want to discuss this first because if you think I will hand the keys to a million-dollar secret, stop reading now. There is no magic path or business plan which can be a carbon copy for success. Every patient is different. Every healthcare worker is different. Every invention is diverse. Every business market is different. So your journey is different than mine and many others as well. I started CathWear in 2012. It's now 2020, and I've yet to buy myself a cup of coffee from any profit coming from CathWear. We just keep putting the money right back into the business. If someone would have told me in 2012, "You're gonna go eight years, and you're still not going to be a multi-millionaire," I wouldn't have believed it! Making it rich is what everybody thinks when you invent something. It is erroneous to think wealth is a guarantee, and it is a consensus (and horrible assumption) that you're going to be a millionaire. The compensation is in the journey. I've grown so much in the journey. I've met so many patients who are struggling with their healthcare and health complications. I've been on the phone with patients, and they're in tears. I'm in tears, listening to their stories about how much CathWear has helped them or their loved one(s). I recall one particular family member had stage four renal cancer, and because of CathWear, they were able to go on a vacation one last time as a family. The patient didn't want to go because of leg bags. His wife called just to say, "Thank you!" I remember bawling my eyes out as I hung up the phone. Up until that point, I sat in this bubble of trying to make it big. I was trying to make a splash or leave my mark. At the end of the day, what we should be doing is trying to improve healthcare. We do this by laying down our ideas like a brick and building on the foundations set before us. There are many ways to find funding when embarking on the entrepreneurial journey.

This book's focus is to talk about the journey and some of the complexities I experienced in starting a business, like the relationship with my business partners, and how important it is to know not everybody has the same passion within the project. Not everyone will have the same goals and aspirations you do, and that's certainly okay. It isn't everyone's desire, within the project, to focus on patients and to improve their quality of life. Some people are motivated by money, and others are inspired by making an impact on patient care. The best projects are when the team originates with these types of people, so one side is pulling left, and the other side is pulling right, yet the result is you are on a straight path to success.

When I invented CathWear, the vision came to me in the operating room. I was working in the operating room. I used to assist the doctors in placing the drains. I saw a patient getting on to the procedure table with his leg bags exposed, and I received a vision for medical underwear designed for patients struggling with wearing leg bags. It's humiliating for a patient. I had the vision, but I was doing it all on my own. I presented it to a friend, Hector Arce—another nurse. He decided to join me on the project. We agreed to split all of the finances, which were out of pocket, 50/50. Hector and I were in nursing school together and had spent time in friendship before classes started. After speaking with him at length, we both decided we didn't want to leave the clinical setting. So, he and his girlfriend added a key feature onto CathWear, which sparked my creative juices to continue designing CathWear to encompass all drains attached to a leg bag. Their addition to the design unlocked the rest of the features and benefits for me. At this point, I started thinking of every dream possible for developing this groundbreaking medical device.

Hector and I knew we didn't want to do anything business-related. We didn't desire to work with numbers, track books, or be salesmen. We didn't want to negotiate deals. Business is numbers-driven. Companies tend to comprise of tangible things and less on emotion. It's about projections and trajectory. I've mentioned that business areas can be a weak area, I believe, for many nurses. We are naturally emotionally-driven, which is what helps us connect with our patients. In the world of entrepreneurship, emotion will get in the way of making the appropriate and best decisions for your company and or project(s). It is critical to balance your team with someone that sees the opposite of you in a situation. We needed someone who did not want to do anything clinically related and did not want to focus on patient care. We waited for the right opportunity, but the patients we were able to help struggled because our idea came to a halt. We needed someone whose strength was our weakness. I realized what I was doing was compartmentalizing the project. Often, when you're going to embark on a journey like this, your mind naturally wants to think you have to do it all by yourself. In reality, you have to break it down into categories of areas of strengths and areas of weaknesses and hire your weaknesses. The ability to identify this was when I started to see myself becoming successful in this business venture.

I ended up speaking with my childhood, Edwin Alvarez, in a series of conversations over a short amount of time concerning developing a contract to bring on someone we were working with as a potential investor. Edwin presented all of the information to me was unique in fashion because he would ask me questions based on what I needed instead of telling me what I was going to need. This method showcased his level of expertise and intelligence within the business world. I found this to be one of the most exciting and attractive ways for someone to interview for a position by merely creating value for his knowledge. It was clear to me we needed to bring him on board, and it was also easy to partner with him because we grew up together. I trusted him, and I knew he would be hungry to succeed along the business venture.

We ended up hiring Edwin, who has his master's degree in business. He didn't want anything to do with nursing and is by no means emotionally- driven, which made Edwin the perfect fit. Time would prove he was completely opposite of me. Edwin was able to take this patented idea, now sitting on the shelf, and turn it into an international business, helping patients across the earth. Edwin's most exciting part coming onto the team was the two days he requested to think about joining us. I didn't realize his ability to research exceptionally well. Over these two days, Edwin had tried to debunk the innovative design of our invention. After the two days had gone by, he came back. He said, "I thought I was going to crush all of your hopes and dreams by showing you there were other products similar to your invention, and I have looked and looked but have not been able to find anything as innovative as this medical underwear." He went on to tell us that he was shocked that somebody had not yet created an invention such as this one. Edwin was now convinced and willing to come along for the ride.

Another interesting point he made was when he said, "I looked at all of the negative reviews from all of the competitors, and it looks like somebody made a product based off of the negative reviews. The design has turned every negative review as an essential feature and benefit within the design for patients." Edwin is not easy to impress, and this was a sure sign we were onto something great.

As we went along the journey, I didn't realize Hector's focus shifted to no longer being part of the project but advancing his nursing career into an acute care setting. Initially, this was difficult for me to understand because it wasn't clear how someone could turn away from such a fantastic journey we were about to begin. Understanding his thought process was one of the hardest things I had to learn--to accept other people's visions and goals for their own life and how they may be different from mine. It was hard for me to navigate this type of environment because nurses are emotionally-driven. The ability to connect emotionally with people is why we are nurses because we can care for patients and let our emotions blend into our profession. We can go above and beyond, but in business, it is likely to be a "nobody cares" type of environment, and I learned the hard way how true this was. At the same time, this is what is so exciting about new beginnings, especially when impacting healthcare. It's a high-risk, high-reward calling, and it is so motivating. You leave yourself with no chance but to succeed. I was able to use my weaknesses and push myself higher in life and go against the tide. I was perfectly okay with being challenged, and I learned early in life that I work extremely well under pressure. I prefer it. I honestly believe and know that hard work does pay off, and the focus was on working as hard as I could on this project. I made a personal commitment not to let anyone outwork me on my project, and this is a tool I used to help me fight the fear of failure and excel in every step along the way. I knew that if I worked harder than anyone else, my weaknesses would be engulfed by my strengths and work ethic, rendering them powerless over my ability to lead the company. I have never believed in luck, as it does not exist--only work ethic. I knew once patients, nurses, caregivers, and doctors saw the innovative design of CathWear, they would be impressed by how it would help their patients. That was my entire goal, getting it into the patients' hands and letting them speak for themselves, which has its weight in gold. You could have a different method to motivate you, and I encourage you to do whatever it takes to win.

"Winners Win." -Eric Thomas

Once Edwin came on board with the team, we started working closer together, as Hector slowly started drifting away. He ended up joining the military and becoming active in the Navy so he could pursue his CRNA. Now, he's become a silent partner. If someone had told me in 2012 that I would start this venture without Hector, I just wouldn't have believed him.

It is critical to understand that your journey's vision and passion must come from within you and never be from outside sources. The people you start with may not be who you end up with as you reach new heights within the journey. When you seek satisfaction and approval outside of yourself, it is very, very deadly and will hinder your plans more than anything else. I believe this is why a lot of ideas don't manifest into actual products.

We patented our idea in July 2013, and in October 2013, entered the Merrimack Valley Sandbox invention contest. We won first place and a fan favorite! The name we chose for this specific contest was "Drainage Partners." Nobody liked the name, but we needed something to enter the competition. Hector and I only had two weeks to prepare for this contest. The chance of presenting was given to us at the last minute. The contest required a company name to enter the competition, and this was the best we could do at the time. During the contest's judging phase, one of the critiques was they liked the idea, but we needed to find a better name for it. After the contest, we had a line of patent attorneys waiting to speak with us. Competing in this event was a fantastic feeling. Also, we were told, "if you open the business and create a market for it, there'll be a bigger payout than if you just try to license the idea." But we didn't want to open the business. So, we tried to license the idea. I called places that were manufacturers of the leg bags (Medline, Merit, Bard, etc.) because we were solving a complication they were creating for patients. Nobody wanted to take CathWear onboard, which highlights something which I have repeated already and will continue to repeat throughout this book--you are the one who has to be the catalyst for your vision. You cannot let anyone hinder your walk based on what they see or don't see for your invention(s).

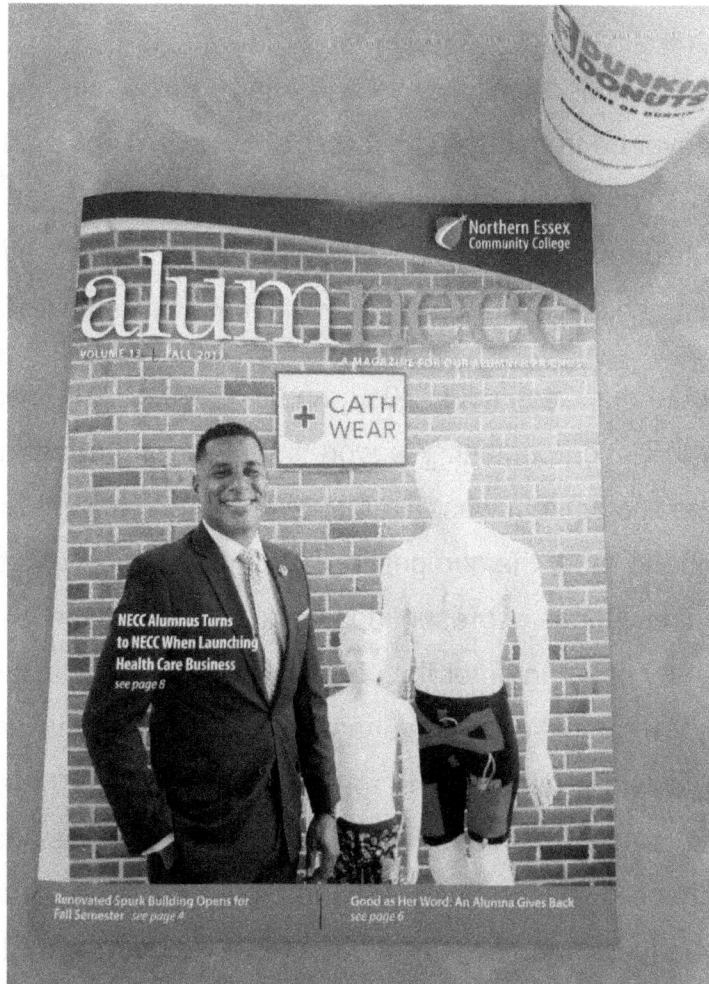

Fortunately for us, the leg bag management industry is a very under-managed market, meaning there are not many innovative ideas out there. Somebody created the leg bag was in the 1960s. The latest innovation to help manage; it was a velcro or elastic strap, which becomes unsanitary and puts the patient at many risks for infection and injury. That's why CathWear, I believe, has been so successful. The name's history started with Hector, who came up with an acronym, C.A.T.H.wear (Catheter Assisted Therapeutic Healing). I thought this was very clever and helped us move away from Drainage Partner. Edwin came along and removed the acronym portion of the name, and I added the capital "W" to make a clear distinction between the two words within the name.

Our logo design came from an idea that Edwin had to reach back to the local community college I had initially graduated from in our hometown (Northern Essex Community College). We reached out to their graphics design class and created a logo design contest for two hundred dollars in the hopes of not only saving money, allowing someone to advance their career. After almost a dozen students submitted their logo design, we picked the one we currently have now by a student whose last name happened to be, Miracle. We liked the medical cross sitting at the center of what looks like a pocket with stitching, symbolizing the number one feature in our patented medical underwear. The proceeds from the contest were used by her (Miracle) to purchase software equipment to open up her own business, and we found this to be so exhilarating and in a "cycle of life" fashion. Months later, we would be on the cover of the NECC magazine as an emerging medical innovator from their school, which was pretty cool to see yourself on the cover of a magazine. Distribution circulated to every school alumni, and people were texting and calling me, saying that I showed up in their mailbox. The opportunity was a great experience that happened to me in my community.

To survive as a nurse entrepreneur, you will have to morph into this business mind while maintaining your love for the profession of nursing. For example, I would come across patients who couldn't afford CathWear, and I would give them out for free as "samples." I would also give samples to potential leads I was trying to develop. My heart is to help people, yet my mind needed to focus on growing a company, and in turn, building a brand. My team would emphasize and say things like, "If you keep giving these away for free, how much longer do you think we'll be in business?" Nursing school never taught us how to be entrepreneurs. The concept of owning your own business is never even touched on during school. Now, I see this as a critical part of nursing. It can be frustrating and intimidating, navigating the business world. The only message expressed in school is 'bedside or bust,' which is an excellent time for the nursing profession to highlight the ability to expand nurses into the corporate world and make an even more enormous impact on patient care.

CHAPTER 1:
NURSES AT THE FOREFRONT OF INNOVATION

Although this chapter's heart concerns nurses, it would be unprofessional not to mention doctors and their healthcare role. We certainly cannot diminish the role of a physician in the care and treatment of a patient. The same also goes for nursing. No one can discredit the role and impact of a nurse in healthcare. They go hand-in-hand.

I believe what we see right now is the nursing profession's emergence to a level never seen before. It has always been the physicians, researchers, and scientists making these groundbreaking changes. 2020 is the decade we are starting to see a massive emergence of nurse innovators, nurse inventors, and nurse entrepreneurs. Nurses need to understand their role in the innovation process because we are so close to patients. We spend more time with patients than physicians, X-ray techs, respiratory techs, or the lab when they come in and draw samples. It's the nurses. We're there.

I was in the United States Air Force after high school, and after the Air Force, I came home. I didn't want anything to do with college when I graduated high school because I knew I would waste the opportunity by living the party life I was accustomed to at that time. Yet after the Air Force, I came with a different mind frame. I decided to enroll in college. I started by setting short-term goals for myself. The best way to achieve long-term goals is to set up a series of short term goals and accomplish them as milestones. At the age of 21, I came up with this "checklist" for myself. By 23, I planned enrollment in college. By 25, I wanted to be in a degree program, and by 27, I wanted to have graduated. While I was going to school, I wanted to be working in the medical field actively. It worked out exactly the way I planned it. By the age of 23, I said that I wanted to enroll back in school, and I did. I took a phlebotomy class, and I got my first A. When I got my first A, I wanted more because I realized I could be successful in school when I was focused and applied myself. It was the most significant motivation because my senior year in high school didn't end so well. I signed up for more classes and completely fell in love with the concept of going to school. It gave me the power to know that I was in control of my career, and I didn't have to work at a job that I didn't like for the rest of my life just to survive.

After working in the laboratory as a phlebotomist for some time, I became a medical assistant. I still wasn't satisfied with my current job roles, and I wanted more for my career. I enrolled in the Radiology Technologist program at the local community college (Northern Essex Community College). I recall being too excited to embark on a medical imaging journey. I had come across the profession of being a radiology technologist as I was working in the laboratory, which is why I wanted to work in the medical field while going to school. I graduated top of my class as I excelled in clinical and in the classroom as well. The knowledge required to remember all anatomical points was a strength of mine, given that I am a visual learner. The best way to describe the difference between radiology and nursing is that you have to know a lot about one thing in radiology. In nursing, you have to know a little about everything when you initially start.

I had no idea what the nursing profession was about and what it entailed. I had heard of a nurse before, but the possibility and thought were so far from my mind that it was a foreign concept. It was like being a brain surgeon--something untouchable for me at the time. When I graduated with my associate's degree in Radiology, I realized I had made a horrible mistake. I didn't know you couldn't obtain a bachelor's degree in Radiology. The only degree available was a degree in management, and this was an area of no interest for me. I assumed everything in the medical field, especially a prestigious career field such as Radiology, that you could get a bachelor's degree. I remember feeling like I hit a glass ceiling at that moment. Within Radiology, I wanted to see what else I could do to maximize the degree's potential and grow within my chosen career field. I noticed diagnostic radiology, CAT scan, and MRI were all lateral moves. Here is what I mean. If you work in diagnostic radiology and go into CAT scan, a significant portion of what you've learned doesn't transfer over into CAT scan. You have to learn a whole new skill set. If you're a CT tech and go into MRI, you have to utilize now an entirely new skill set--not much transfers over. If you are a female radiology technologist and you work in mammography, you have to use a different skill set because none of the knowledge transfers over. I ended up cross-training into interventional radiology, an operating room setting where I would get to scrub in during procedures and get a closer role in treating a patient, which was my (unknown at the time) burning desire. Going into an operating room setting was the best thing for me to grow within the degree. This decision will remain the greatest one for my medical career because it gave me exposure to a nurse's role and the profession's significance upon patient care. I hadn't worked with nurses in this capacity, and I was in for the introduction of an entirely new world. It was awesome!

While working as a radiology technologist, my role was to set up the room in the procedure table with all of the sterile equipment needed for each procedure scheduled. The hospital where I was working was a teaching hospital, and a lot of the time, it was a resident who would scrub in on the procedure, leaving me left out of the very reason I took the job--more involvement in the patient's care. After the room was prepared and set up for the procedure, my responsibilities as a radiology technologist finished unless the interventional radiologist needed more equipment, which morphed my role into a "float" or like a scrub tech. I believe this provided a significant impact on my very young career despite not being challenged. It consisted of maintenance and service within a procedure instead of direct patient care. Feeling unchallenged left me in the same predicament as when I worked in the laboratory, wanting more out of my medical career and still desiring to spend more time directing patient care.

As all of this was unfolding within my career, I had a front-row seat to the nurses meeting the patient and immediate family members, assessing the patient before the procedure, giving medications, starting IVs, and then recovering the patient post-procedure. I would see nurses reading a patient's chart, and I had no idea what they were even doing. It piqued my interest, and I would think, "Man, what are they doing?" For me, as a tech, I was missing something. I was missing patient interaction--the professional intimacy. I decided to go back to school for nursing and earn my baccalaureate degree. My responsibilities within the operating room setting didn't compare because the more I watched the nurses work, it highlighted my current role, which focused on cleaning the room, turning it over, and starting the process for the next procedure as aforementioned all over again. The only thing that stuck out to me about nurses is that nurses are "mean," which most people working in a hospital setting believe and think.

I became good friends with a male nurse in our department. He happened to live within a few miles from my home. We started hanging out two or three times a week and also started taking on-call shifts together. We started talking about what each other gets paid, and I concluded he was getting double the pay compared to what I was getting paid. We were in the same room, with the same patient, but he would have a different interaction with the patient than I would. When we got called into the hospital, he would go to the ER and get the patient. I would just be setting up the room, setting up the sterile tray, and getting all the equipment for the doctor. I just felt a big void within my career choice. I went back to nursing school two years after I graduated with my degree in Radiology. More involvement in patient care is what I desired. I had a thirst for more knowledge and growth. Nursing was the release valve. Nursing was the solution to everything I wanted within my medical career.

I remember being so excited to go back to school and be enrolled in the nursing program. There was a long waitlist at the University of Massachusetts. I believe, because I was a male Hispanic nurse, there was an opportunity for me to be selected ahead of the others, so the nursing body of students represented the community in which we lived. Male nurses are critical in advancing the nursing profession, and I am convinced that this was the reason Hector and I bypassed the waitlist. I was so excited for my future! I was so happy to spend time with patients. I started getting along more with the nurses in my department. I started spending time with them as they read their patients' charts, got into medications, and looked at drug interactions. It was just a whole new world I was eager to explore. I felt honored when I would tell people I enrolled in nursing school. I thought I had taken control of my career and was no longer in a position of complaining but more in a place of doing something about it. I was motivated by the response I would get when I told people I was in nursing school. These responses let me know how prestigious the career field is. I was quickly experiencing how important it was to push yourself from within to achieve a career you love. That is what nursing was for me. It was my opportunity to rise to a professional level to help people and impact their lives from many different perspectives.

The ability to impact a human's life is the main reason why nurses are so critical in bringing inventions and innovations. Somebody cannot compare the time we spend with patients in any other role in a clinical setting. We see the plight of the patients we encounter and how they struggle to manage their health complications. Nurses are making the biggest splash in new inventions and innovations because they develop new and practical ways to help patients.

Many times people have inventions already in their minds or innovations that they are not putting into practice because it's not as big as someone else's idea--it's not the cure for cancer, or because "it's never going to sell." You could have a billion-dollar idea. You could have a one million dollar idea. You could have a couple hundred thousand dollars a year idea. Moments of failure in any aspect of life is almost inevitable, and there is certainly no way for you to prepare for how much you will experience throughout your entrepreneurial journey. You are obligated to push forward with your idea or innovations because the focus has to be on patient care and not the dollar value, which will only benefit you. We need to realize that we are doing an enormous disservice to patient care if we don't follow through with our ideas. We need it. We need you. We need the innovations that you have to help patients on a holistic level. For example, CathWear helps patients with leg bags, but what you have could help patients with something different to manage a different and unique problem. The times we're currently living in is the most significant time for nurses to take advantage of the opportunities due to the professional influence nurses have in many different areas. Nurses are also transcending into other industries because we are the number one trusted profession making us well-positioned to meet market demands and start a new business. Four or five nurses putting their innovative ideas forward can completely shift the healthcare trajectory of a patient. The important thing is not whether one makes $10 million, $1 million, or even just $100 from the business venture. The essential things are patients growing, nurses growing and propelling the industry forward, and improving patient care and outcomes.

Nurses at the forefront are so critical, especially now, with everything we've seen with the COVID-19. We are essentially a medical firefighter. We always use stories of the firefighters running into a burning building when everybody's running out. That's what it felt like during this COVID-19 pandemic. I have never been more proud to be a nurse as I watched nurses respond to COVID-19. It was like watching 100 firefighters running into a burning building. I saw nurses leaving their hometown going to work in the hot zones. I'm from Boston, Massachusetts. COVID-19 turned into a war zone here, New York, and other parts of America's northeast region. People were dropping like flies, and the cases were increasing faster than most areas in the country. The city I currently lived in was one of Massachusetts's hardest hit, and in turn, the most stringent sanctions.

We are the ones who spend the most time with the patient. True, someone is putting the patient under anesthesia and intubating the patient. The respiratory therapist is using the monitor, and we need them. Yes, the doctors are coming, and they are giving the diagnosis. That's all great. But when the patient is there and is lying in bed and doesn't have the X-ray tech, a respiratory therapist, a doctor, or even their family, it's nurses. We are there talking to them, putting our problems aside, our home complications aside, our family struggles aside, problems with our children aside, and even some capacity, people struggling with alcohol and drug addictions. That's how critical nurses are. The ability to be selfless is why we need to realize our role in bringing inventions and innovations to the market. I remember reading somewhere on social media that said something along the lines of, "You signed up to be a nurse, so stop complaining--you're on the forefront of COVID-19."

This person was right. We did sign up for this. We are the ones who are closest to these patients. We are the ones who are forsaking our own lives to be with them. We deserve more recognition within the health field than we currently get. The only way to advance the nursing profession is for more nurses to overcome their fear of failure, push beyond the bedside, and step into the corporate world. That's how critical nursing is.

It is very dangerous for a nurse to enter into the corporate world without balancing the desire to go above and beyond, giving it all your heart, and making some decisions based on non-emotional logic to be successful. The lessons I learned from opening my own business have transcended into personal areas of my life and helped me grow in places I didn't know were lacking. I had to learn to have a sound business mind and deal with people who hadn't had the chance to grasp the concept of patient care.

Before leaving this chapter, I would like to make a brief comment about male nurses. I never imagined having any difficulty becoming a nurse, and I wanted to share some things which happened to me with the hopes of breaking a century-old barrier, which is the role of a man within the nursing profession. During my maternity-pediatric rotation in nursing school, I experienced the most incredible difficulty in my career. It was very subtle but also a very overwhelming feeling to think that I was in the wrong place and at the wrong time. While in the maternity ward, I needed to assess a postpartum patient. I felt very overwhelmed during the situation because I respected this person's privacy, particularly at this moment in time in their life. My clinical instructor walked into the room and asked the patient if it was okay for a male student to come and do the assessment, to which the patient agreed. However, I didn't necessarily agree, and I reluctantly walked into the room.

The instructor wanted me to assess the lochia accumulated on the absorbent pad, which was still placed on the patient lying in bed. As the instructor spoke to me about lochia, she wanted me to lean over the patient enough to see the vaginal opening and the lochia. I leaned over briefly and made pretend that I assessed the area and quickly stood upright again. I could feel my heart rate increasing, and I was starting to sweat because I thought I was violating the patient's privacy and that a man shouldn't be placed with this type of patient at this particular time in their life. My clinical instructor noticed my brief observation and firmly stated in front of the patient to lean over and get my head as close as possible and observe the lochia to do a proper assessment. It was at this moment that I knew I was going to have a tough time in nursing.

Then there was a second patient on the same day of this clinical rotation. If the previous patient allowed me to make this private assessment, unquestionably, this next patient would also. I walked into the room, and my clinical instructor treated the patient. Immediately after, as I was walking in, I greeted the patient and introduced myself. On the other side of the patient's bed, Unbeknownst to me, was the patient's husband sleeping on a hospital mat. At the sound of my voice, he shot up off his mat onto his knees and looked directly at me as I walked in to see the patient. I can still remember the look on his face, and I can visualize it as I'm writing this sentence. He looked at me with a protective look over his wife, which I could certainly understand. The patient was very cold towards me and never made eye contact as I did the assessment and spoke in a low tone. Her body language alone let me know she was not comfortable with me coming back. After we left the room, I pleaded with my clinical instructor to please allow me to do other tasks during the day and not let me see any more patients. We had a long discussion in which my clinical instructor agreed that this was the best approach and then began to share her thoughts on men in the maternity rotation and how she was going to petition the school to consider changing their current policy.

I explained that I would be willing to do a double rotation in the emergency room instead of staying in the maternity ward. Let's just say she gave me "light cafeteria duties" for my time there, and I couldn't thank her enough for it.

Nursing is predominantly a woman's profession and has always been this way since the 20th century. However, when I was in the United States Air Force boot camp, we were taught basic life support and the importance of playing the nurse's role on the battlefield. During the many wars experienced through humanity, women were never on the battlefield, treating the wounded, but it was men nursing men. Essentially, men were the first nurses before it became exclusive to women. I would like a male nurse if I was ever in a position where I was a patient, simply because I could speak freely and not feel embarrassed in any way, and I believe many other patients feel the same way, whether male or female. I firmly believe this is why there's such a rapid growth of men in nursing, because of the balance we provide. It is never safe to say one gender is better than another at any task, yet God designed men and women to do different equal strength things. Nursing provides a balance where males and females can work together simultaneously for a common goal, which is improved healthcare for all. Men in nursing are similar to women becoming CEOs and Fortune 500 business owners, and both are moving away from their stereotypes placed by society. It's about the right person for the right job, and this has to be a symbiotic interaction within all professions.

Men who decide to become nurses have generally been given dishonor among other men (and possibly women) as being weak. As society grows in understanding, we realize that there is power in weakness because men and women are making healthcare strong.

CHAPTER 2:
FAILURES AND OBSTACLES

Unfortunately, most people identify with failures more than they identify with success stories. It's not often that you can share a success story with someone in a circle of people and other people understand what you mean. It's just the way it is because a lot of people understand failure, pain, and regret. Transparency about our losses is a way to reach and identify with people at any level to engage, and then show them how they too can overcome--overcoming in all areas, both in your professional life and in your personal life. I say that because I had a failure, which I used to help me overcome the stresses of starting my next invention. It has been the catalyst for me throughout my career: never to quit and never listen to negativity when I'm going to start a project. At the moment, I own seven patents. Six US patents and one European patent, and none of those are from my first invention. I also have a patent-pending for a modification that I designed. My first invention was a complete failure. My son was two months old, and his nasal passage was significantly blocked. We thought he was going to die in his sleep because he was having trouble breathing at night. It sounded like his nose was very congested. It seemed as if he just needed to blow his nose, and he would have slept better. The blue suction device they give you in the maternity ward didn't have a strong enough suction to remove all the mucus. We're not going to make an infant two months old blow their nose. We stayed up watching him at night and making sure he was breathing throughout his sleep. I wanted to do something about it. I needed to do something about it. So I went into the operating room the next day and grabbed a yankauer suction device from the wall, and I also cut off a two-foot piece of tubing for it. I went home and connected the yankauer to the tubing. The anchor's end has a bulb on it, so it doesn't go inside the nasal passage. It sits outside of the nose and creates a seal. I blocked the other nare with my finger, so only one nostril was open with the yankauer suction device pressed against it. I cut the tubing long, and I would suck the mucus out of my son's nose. The mucus wouldn't go into my mouth because the tubing was so long. It would just stay trapped in the distal portion of the yankauer tubing.

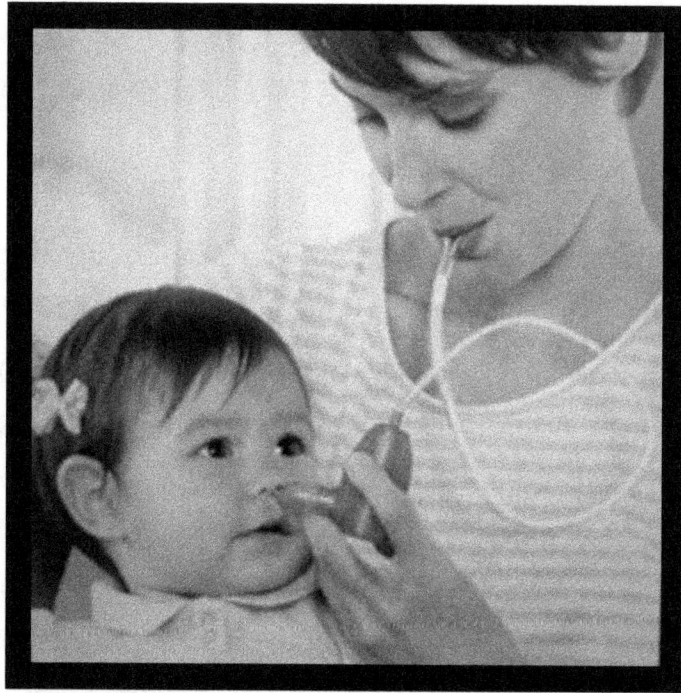

I would then switch sides and do the same thing. Our son, finally, slept like a baby--pun intended. I remember being very excited and feeling like this should be invented for others to use. I wanted to invent it. The greatest mistake you can make when you want to invent something is to start seeking approval from other people, and that's what I did. I started showing it to people in my life during this time, and I was told it was stupid. I was told it wasn't going to work. I showed it to my son's pediatrician. The pediatrician discouraged me. She said, "Oh, well, you have to get a patent, and those take years. It's going to take, you know, over $10,000, and it's going to take so much time. You have to get FDA approval because it's going inside the nose, and the nasal passage is so close to the brain. It's just not worth it. You know, it's good you're using it for your son, but it's not something worth patenting." All I kept thinking to myself was, "But it doesn't go inside of the nose! It sits outside of the nasal passage!" Her comments took the wind out of my sail. I remember just feeling so defeated. The discouragement I felt was like someone kicked over my sandcastle. I was so proud I had completed inventing the suction device, but I gave up. When I gave up about a year later, someone sent me a picture of this same invention. It was on the shelves at Walmart because someone else invented it after I did. It was tough for me to accept that I had failed because I had given up. I decided to listen to people. I decided to seek the approval of others. I decided to apply outside negativity to my life and invention.

When you're inventing something, it is imperative to remind yourself that you are the driving force. You understand your invention better than anyone else simply because it is your creativity. You shouldn't allow someone else to push your vision. It's your responsibility as the innovator, as the inventor. You have to be the one that says, "I know the benefit of this because I'm the one who created it!" It has to be you! You do this by avoiding and refusing to listen to negativity while realizing it's going to be a long, long road. I used the failure to quit on my first invention to propel me in every area of my life. It was that impactful when I saw the picture of it for sale on the shelf. Remembering our failures is how we can turn mistakes into a positive event in our business ventures (and life). There is a healthy way to recognize errors. Pain is a great teacher. Pain pushes us into our purposes in life. It was no longer a mistake but fuel for the engine. I was going to self-motivation for a long time. I keep a picture of it in the gallery images on my phone. Anytime I want to quit, or anytime I'm feeling discouraged, I look at that specific photo. I say to myself, "I don't want anybody ever to invent something I was supposed to invent because I decided to quit."

As nurse innovators, nurse inventors, and nurse entrepreneurs, it is essential that we be the driving force within the vision. Once you establish yourself as the lead person on the project, you become the team's catalyst. As you start to build your team, they will become catalysts, which will allow everyone to help each other along the way. It's always your responsibility to keep pushing forward. You cannot let the responsibility of putting in the most amount of work for the project to be placed on someone else. Every organization has one leader who bears the brunt of it all. It is always your responsibility to keep the dream alive. The best way to do this is to realize the life obstacles that will come whether you invent or don't. Roadblocks are always going to be there. Once you realize no matter what you do, whether you quit or don't quit, life is still challenging. So why not push through all of this? Why not overcome the personal problems we have outside of our professional career? I dealt with a lot of personal circumstances, such as addiction. I went through a horrible divorce, and I still decided to push through. All of those things can derail a dream, or you can also use the setbacks in life to move you into your greater purpose-- pain pushes purpose. You learn how to manage those better, and as they come, you can absorb the impact much better to the point where no momentum is lost. Nothing can get in your way. Well, it can get in your way, but it won't move you from your path. The best way to push forward is to keep this thought in your head: patients need your ideas. It's not about making millions of dollars and living life on a yacht. It's not about us. It's about the patient. There's no joy in just helping yourself live a better life or making it all about the money. We are nurses. The fun comes from knowing that you are advancing the nursing profession and impacting patient care.

Maybe you're reading this and going through some struggles with addictions or instability in your home life. I encourage you to keep your mind on the things which are a priority and rise above the noise. Use the dark times to push your professional career to a place where it's never been before.

Another challenge that can make or break an idea is the emphasis on the money needed to start the entrepreneurship journey. Finances are a big obstacle. You would be surprised how many people will invest in a good idea. There are so many programs, incubators, and government grants for early startups, minority-owned, woman-owned, and veteran-owned businesses. Every community has organizations that conduct accelerated programs with cash incentives for completing the two or three months required for their specific programs. There are an enormous amount of small business loans. We cannot let money be a reason to delay the start of our pursuit of making an impact on patient care and pushing our inventions and innovations forward. Many companies fail because they start giving away equity in the company early instead of seeking free money. By the time the company begins to grow, the company shares have started to dissipate. Everything costs money: a mortgage, a car payment, private schools for our children, going out to eat, a particular lifestyle, etc.

Why not invest in your dreams? Why not invest in your business the way we invest in everything else which takes our money? I have met so many people in my life who say things like, "Well, I don't want to go to school because I don't want to have a monthly payment for my student loans." That's one of the silliest things I've ever heard. When you buy a car and drive it off the lot, it immediately depreciates, so a vehicle is not an investment. A college degree makes you more money, making it an investment of your time. You're making more money an hour or per year. Who cares if they take out two hundred dollars from your bank account for the next fifteen years if you're making an extra thousand dollars a week because of your time in school? I highly encourage anyone who is reading this book to consider obtaining their next degree. I want to be clear: it's not about the degree, and it's not about the title, but it is about the ambition and the push of innovation. We need to realize that we spend so much money on garbage that we cannot quit our dreams because of not having the finances available when we start a business. We didn't have any money for CathWear, and as we started the project, money just started showing up everywhere. Every time we needed money, it just started showing up in a multitude of different directions. I'll be discussing this in more detail later on in the book. I will break down the different ways we could bring money in for CathWear, and I want you to realize you can do this same thing.

I worked in the operating room when I saw a patient come in with a nephrostomy bag clipped with a safety pin to his underwear. This patient was about to get on the procedure table when I walked into the room. I immediately had a vision of medical underwear, which we would later call "CathWear" (the formal name came years after the vision). I originally designed it a lot different than what it looks right now. As the saying goes, "If you're not embarrassed by your first prototype, then you launched too late." I was in the United States Air Force, and I have excellent attention to detail. I also can draw exceptionally well. After work one day, I went home and drew pictures of CathWear from different angles and perspectives. As time passed, I went to Walmart and purchased long-spandex boxer brief men's underwear. I also made a stop at the local arts and craft store to purchase Velcro, sewing thread, and extra cloth material for the features, which would turn out to be a groundbreaking design in the medical garment industry. My stepmother, Rosa Mohika, seamstress, made prototypes at her kitchen table for approximately two years, giving them out to patients to obtain feedback on the innovative design.

I had inquired into a company called "InventHelp" after seeing their commercial on television. I took this as a sign for me to push forward and develop this medical device. InventHelp helped us file for the patent on the design. We obtained 15 utilities within the patent, and they provided us with some market analysis, which, looking back, I can see was very superficial. The market analysis didn't help us at all. We were young in the project then and in life. We thought all information given to us regarding the patent had value to help us grow. The marketing material provided to us seemed minimal, with little sophistication in its presentation. Still, at the same time, it was the marketing we needed to show us what it was going to take to become entrepreneurs.

I was in the backyard of our home one day having a fire when Hector showed up. He began to ask me about the invention and where I was in the process. I had no idea Hector would ask me a question that would change my career trajectory (and my life) forever. He asked me if he could go half on the entire project with me. Honestly, I didn't have the fifteen thousand dollars, nor did I have the money to make the monthly payment required either. The meeting with Hector was a divine appointment that walked right into my backyard, and I couldn't and didn't resist. I knew I would need some help, but I didn't realize where it would come from or what type of support I would need. From this day forward, we split CathWear on all associated costs 50/50. Hector and his girlfriend added a couple of features to it, giving me ideas for more features to add. I'm not going to lie, but I felt jealous when adding the Catheter Channel Track on CathWear. I felt like they made my invention better than I had initially thought. Instead of getting into my feelings and allowing my emotions to overcome me, I decided to use it as motivation to add more features to the design. I didn't want someone else to come after us and make the changes we could've made at this stage. I then designed it to encompass all drains: nephrostomy, biliary, suprapubic, and Foley drains.

I designed my invention based on the critique of a nurse. Now at the time, I was inventing this, I was a Radiology Technologist, and I looked at it through the eyes of a nurse. I was also in my first year of nursing school. I thought of every possible way a nurse would try to discredit my invention. I used this technique based on what I saw from nurses and what they are highly critical of, and rightfully so when it comes to presenting products to their patients. I attempted to discredit CathWear, and everything which I knew somebody would try to say was why it didn't work; I turned that into a feature. If a nurse said, "Well, this impedes the flow of gravity, because now the bag is affixed to the thigh," my sales pitch would be that it does not impede the flow of gravity, and I would show the Catheter Channel Track and how it all points down into the pocket. If a nurse said, "The underwear would cause perspiration and then irritate the patient's skin," I responded by explaining how our material, being a wicking material, was fast-drying, similar to biker shorts. If a nurse said, "My patient is going to have to disconnect the leg bag from the tubing, which would increase the risk of infection," I would respond and say that I designed CathWear. Hence, the patient never has to disconnect the catheter's leg bag, thereby lowering the infection risk.

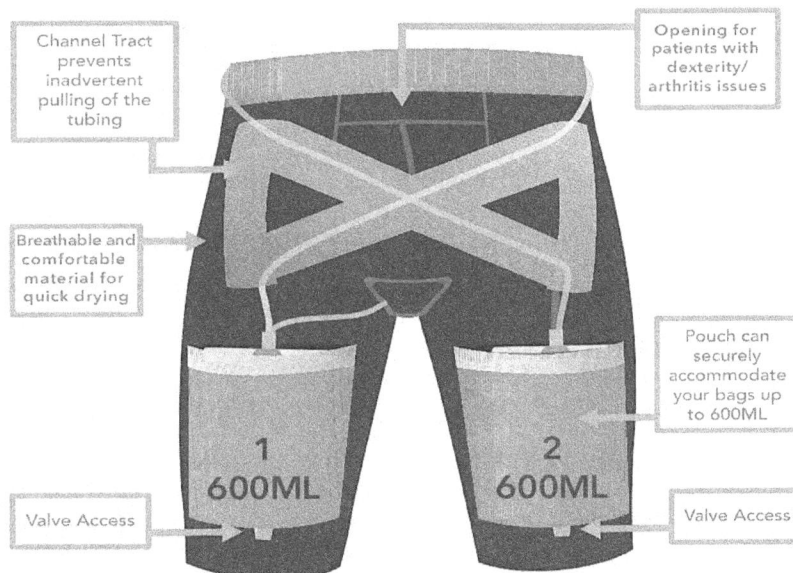

I did this because some of the biggest haters in the medical industry are nurses themselves, and at times, this is what the professional must do, advocate for our patients rightly. The downside is we then happen to complicate things that are quite practical. I met a nurse from one of the largest, oldest, and most prestigious hospitals in the country, found in downtown Boston. I had sent emails for some time and finally was able to get them to agree to a sample. When I went into the hospital to give the nurse practitioner the sample of CathWear, the first words out of her mouth were, "My co-worker says they look bulky in the front." I could've just walked out right then and there while throwing my hands in the air. Instead, I said to her, "You can't go by what someone else says about CathWear unless you assess my product for yourself and measure it against the benefits of the standing competition, which are the elastic straps." Once she opened the package right in front of me, she then went on to say how sleek it felt and how it didn't feel bulky at all. I just smiled. We can't keep shooting innovation in the foot before it even walks into the door, which nurses tend to be the biggest proponents of doing this exact thing. I have had to convince more nurses to try CathWear than anyone else. One nurse told me the urine would reflux back into the patient's bladder and cause an infection. I went on to say to her that all leg bags have a one-way valve that prevents this from happening. In the middle of the in-service, and with 20 other nurses in the room, she made one of them go and grab a leg bag, fill it with water and had me prove it to her on the spot. We have to be smarter with accepting innovations where we are not also a hindrance.

I then added other openings and features to encompass all medical drains, which would require a leg bag. I wanted to design it so nobody could come after us and make it better, and the only way to do that was to continue critically thinking through each phase of the design from a patient quality of life perspective. I was so motivated by the changes made; it propelled CathWear into the greatest medical undergarment the medical industry has ever seen. We wanted to focus on patient comfort and improved quality of life by mitigating the complications associated with wearing a light bag. We designed it to replace the patient's regular underwear, and we knew this would require quality craftsmanship, detail, and material, so we did just that.

Your thought process has to get creative because this is what you do when you don't have money. You fight through it. You find people who want to join the journey with you, and you put your ideas and finances together. You find ways to push forward. You have enough obstacles in life as it is, so don't let money be one of them because patients need your ideas.

You cannot let money be a reason not to start your pursuit of making an impact on patient care. Why not invest in a dream? Why not invest in your business? You cannot stop because you don't have the finances available when you start a business. I simply can't emphasize it enough.

In addition to money, another obstacle is time management. Time management is so critical. I don't think you ever truly master it. Most of us go in and out of phases, and if you can master it at a high level, then hats off to you, but it starts to get more complicated the higher up you go in the entrepreneurial kingdom. Quite frequently, people don't want to take the time to focus on the business. I have spoken to so many business owners who have said the same thing regarding time management. Most will say that it is challenging to balance time for a business, time with family, or even life in general. There are times when building my business caused strife in my family. The same has happened to some of my business partners as well. I have had to step away from my phone or maybe schedule a call for a different time, such as when the wife and kids are asleep, I'd be up working on my dream. There have been times when I have gone out on a date with my wife. I've had to give up my phone to focus on what truly mattered to me, which was loving her. It was still complicated because I felt every phone call or text message, or email was a potential client or nurse, which I had been engaging in trying to grow the business. I was so determined that nothing was going to stop me. Time management is very crucial because many people don't like the idea that you can't have it all. You can't serve two masters. You can't open up your business and also have a flourishing marriage or parental life. It's either you're feeding one or the other. It's learning to balance. It's kind of like a tennis match. First, you're on this side--wham, you hit the ball. Now you're with the business. Wham, you hit the ball, again! You kind of just bounce back and forth until you end up getting into a good rhythm where you are at equilibrium with all things

35

aforementioned. It is essential to realize that it is going to take some time. Something I often tell my wife and kids is, "The things that I am doing now are for you, so that we may live a better life now and in the future." My words were not necessary to manipulate them in any way per se, yet, at the same time, these are my true intentions. I am doing it for my wife. I am doing it for my kids so we can have a different lifestyle, a better lifestyle. I want to change the financial trajectory of my children for generations. My goal is always to make the most significant impact on anything involving me.

I also want to sacrifice my time for the patients who will benefit from my innovations. You should do this too. When you invest your time, you should realize that you are investing in someone's family member, loved one, a father, a mother, a brother, or a sister who will need your design. You're creating something that is potentially going to make their life better; what better way to advance the nursing profession than by sacrificing your own time for the patients who will need your invention. Balancing everything at this level is vital. You have to be the one to implement the balance of your time. You have to set the tone. You have to figure out when you can carve out time.

You may have to get up two hours before your shift so that you can invest an hour into your business plan in the morning. It may mean spending less time on social media, the computer, television, phone conversations, or maybe for your lunch break; you don't hang out with everyone from your department. When I used to go to lunch, I used to go to lunch by myself. I never sat with my coworkers because that was my time to invest in my dream. It didn't matter if I sat one table away, but I always sat alone at work and school for either of my degrees. I would utilize this time to send emails or text messages or start working on my business plan. Sometimes it may have been just to take a mental break, but I never sat with my coworkers. I didn't care if they would make comments on how I would avoid them during break time. I had a dream, and I was working on it. I focused not on what they were saying or doing. I focused on leaving my mark on patient care and advancing the nursing practice.

We have more time than we think we do. The President of the United States of America has the same 24 hours we do. The world's richest billionaire has the same 24 hours we do. Our time may have to be adjusted to meet the demands of becoming an entrepreneur. There will most likely be something we have to be willing to sacrifice. Something has to give. If you want to go high up in the entrepreneurial kingdom, you're going to have to sacrifice something. What that something is will be different for everyone. It's on an individual basis. It was challenging for me because I used to coach my son's football and baseball teams, and I had to balance that time. When I wasn't coaching, I used to go to my son's games and bring study material with me. I would read my class notes. I was always doing something to push my career and to push myself higher.

When I was in nursing school, I worked on the third shift Radiology department as a diagnostic x-ray tech after earning my degree as a Radiology Technologist. My shift ended at 6:30 in the morning. I would be working on my class assignments throughout the entire shift. The only time I had to work was when a patient requisition would come out of the printer, and it was my turn in the rotation, which wasn't very often during those hours. I wanted to be different than my coworkers. They would spend their free time on social media or using their cell phones. Other coworkers would spend their time watching Netflix throughout the entire shift; I would utilize the time to finish all of my nursing assignments and get all of my studying done all night long, essentially getting paid for it. Working and studying at the same time is what I meant about balancing time. Here is a perfect example of being the driving force behind your time management while pursuing your goals. If I could tell you anything that would help you balance your time, it would be to look at the end goal, changing the thermometer of patient care. The most incredible motivational tool is knowing that you are doing something to better your career to impact patient care.

As I think back to this time, I remember I would have my nursing uniform ironed on a hanger in the back seat of a Honda Pilot, which was our family car. I took the Honda Pilot so that I could put the seats down in the back. I would stop at the gas station to buy a cup of coffee before I parked on campus. I would leave the coffee cup in the cup holder, so I would start drinking it to gain some energy for my clinical rotation when I woke up. I used to set my alarm for two hours and sleep in the back of the car after working the third shift. I would use a bottle of water, toothpaste, and a toothbrush to brush my teeth. Then,

I would get dressed in the car, and I would walk to school. I remember feeling so tired, but still, I used to fight through it. I was awake, ready, and I was learning. I graduated top of my nursing class. I never forgot what I went through while working the third shift. They were already getting tired of continually switching my hours around from week to week. The third shift was the only way I could work and go to nursing school.

Sometimes we create our obstacles. I have met quite a few nurses on LinkedIn in my professional career. I was surprised by some of the things I heard them say about not pushing their idea forward or having trouble starting or growing the project. I believe it's pride. Pride always kills a dream. Pride will kill a dream one million times stronger than any negativity spoken in your direction. A nurse I met on LinkedIn had an invention and was starting to grow the market, but he ran out of steam. He was tired. Although he was already closing distribution channels, he was tired of dealing with things' business side. I suggested getting some help, and the response I got was that the nurse didn't want to give up any part of the company, nor did he have any money to pay anyone for help. I tried to explain to this nurse that you have to pay them with equity if you don't have any money to pay an employee. I was shocked to know that he would rather have the entire piece of the pie and keep his ideas grounded than to give someone a slice. If he would have been willing to give a little, he could have potentially gained a lot.

I met another nurse who had an invention that wasn't doing well. He had a good idea. I decided to connect him with my manufacturer of CathWear. I am a US Air Force Veteran, and I wanted to have CathWear made in the USA, but it wasn't possible. Our current manufacturer is in China. He was very reluctant to speak to someone because they were from China. It was very, very shocking to me because the questions were, "Do they speak English? Will they steal my idea? How can I trust them?". One would think that because they are my manufacturer and I speak English, and I am referring you to them, they speak English. How else would I be communicating with them? How many times do we shut the door on ourselves by placing obstacles which aren't even there? We must understand that sometimes self-created obstacles will sideline our inventions and be a hindrance to patient care. If you don't remove the pride and stigma of branching out and opening yourself up to all possibilities, you won't succeed. Don't create your obstacles.

Lastly, I met another nurse who had an idea and a prototype already built. As we were conversing, the nurse asked me if she should license the idea or open a business. I explained to this nurse that she had a greater chance of success if she would license the idea instead of opening a business. She was telling me how great of an idea it was, and as I was visualizing what she was telling me over the phone, I did believe it was a great idea. She asked me what the difference between licensing and opening a business was. I licensed a surgical clip to Cook Medical in 2014, and I have experience in the licensing process. I helped her understand that you are essentially signing it off to another company that will build, market, distribute, and sell it for you when you license an idea. I had to license my surgical clip. There was not going to be a high success rate because I couldn't do the things needed to promote the design. The steps would include; sterilize the surgical clip with ethylene oxide, having it heat-sealed, and having it shipped deep within a hospital setting in the operating room to get it onto the procedure table. The actual clip itself already existed as a towel clamp in the sterile procedure pack. I modified it and changed its intended use by adding glue and foam pads to it, making it a new invention. I want to repeat this, so it's clear to the reader--i*f you modify something and change its intended use, then it becomes an entirely new invention.*

I can't create a business for this device and then market it to a surgical company. I knew I had to get rid of it by having it licensed. I was willing to give them a large portion of any royalties or proceeds in exchange for the invention's success. I was trying to explain to this nurse to incorporate this same concept for her design. I encouraged this nurse and told her that although they are taking a large portion, they do most of the work.

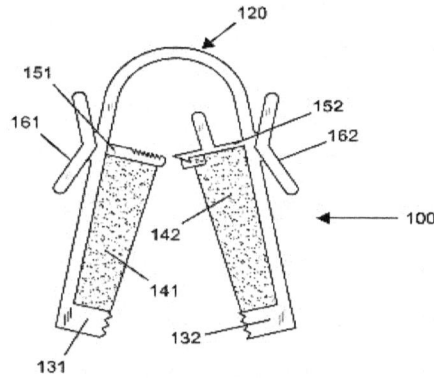

FIG. 1

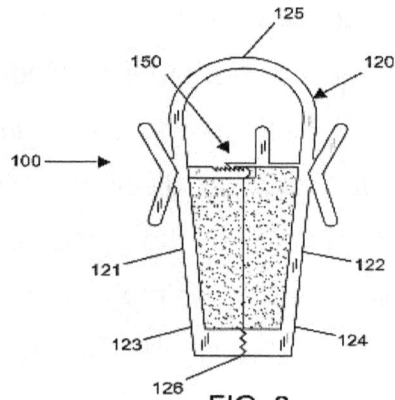

FIG. 2

I further explained that she would still be getting compensated in some capacity and look at the patients who will benefit from her idea and not just the finances. It would be an additional paycheck that could double or triple one's yearly salary and provide a financially comfortable lifestyle. The nurse went on to tell me that she would "never license the idea so that somebody else can make millions of dollars off of her idea while she made pennies." I was utterly shocked by this response. I asked her, "How much is your invention making now?" She said, "Nothing." I explained to her she would instead make zero dollars and not help patients in need than to license it, increase her yearly salary to some capacity, and advance patient care. She repeated her same response. At that moment, I knew that we had a significant problem in healthcare. Decisions like this become a hindrance to nurses becoming the greatest innovators of all time, simply because we do not focus on patient care as much as we are on our ego, titles, and financial stability.

FIG. 3

FIG. 4

FIG. 5

FIG. 6

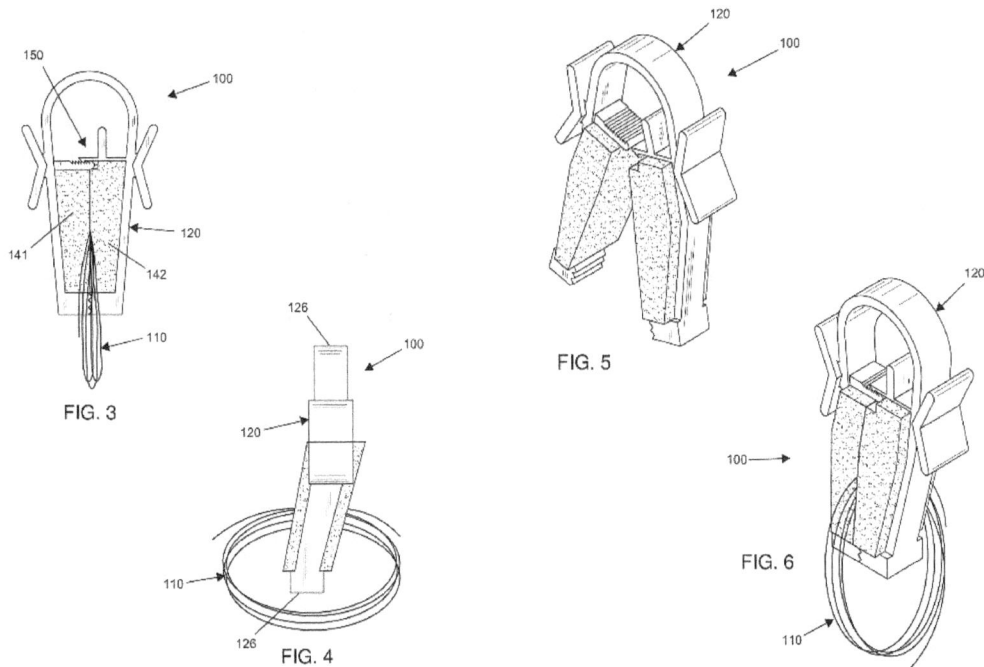

Many times we complicate our journeys. We have to stop getting in our ways and develop a "yes" mentality to better assess things for ourselves. Simply say "yes" to the next step in the process.

I opened my LinkedIn account in October of 2019. I met a lot of nurses who had innovations/ inventions themselves and wanted to know if they should license it or not. The best way to know which one will suit you is pretty simple: how will you get it to the desired patients?

Understanding how the market approach should be is a critical decision because it will give you two entirely different outcomes. As I mentioned above, the surgical clip I invented was tough to get into the operating room on a procedure table. I was able to think this through because of my experience working in an operating room. I saw sales rep after sales rep come in but under the license or contract of a major surgical device company such as Boston Scientific Cook Medical, Terumo, BD. I didn't think I would do that with the surgical clip, so I decided to build prototypes and ship them around to each of those companies.

For me, Cook Medical was the one who saw the benefits. CathWear was an invention where I could build it myself and also build the brand. Underwear is very common, and I thought that selling medical underwear would allow me direct access to patients, so I wouldn't need to license it, although I tried to license it. I'm very thankful for all of those companies who turned down my pitch for a licensing agreement for CathWear because this allowed me to grow the market for a bigger payout later. You have to ask yourself these same questions based on past clinical experience between you and your team.

Another way to create your obstacles is by being disorganized. After I graduated with my radiology degree, I started a job in radiology sales. I worked in radiology on the second shift, and then I had a second job in radiology sales during the day. I wanted to maximize the degree to the best of my ability. I learned so much in medical sales, and little did I know that it would come in handy over a decade down the road when I started working for my own company. I remember working with a sales rep, and the sales rep said that when you walk into someone's office, and you see their desk is messy, it means their mind is cluttered. Your desk is a direct reflection of your mind.

I can always tell how my life is going if I look at my desk's condition when I walk into and out of my office. Often you hear people who have a messy desk say things like, "It's organized confusion." I believe this to be an oxymoron to cover up for being disorganized. I didn't immediately apply this to my life, but it started to take root. As I mentioned before, I was in the Air Force, and this made me very detail-oriented. I am very meticulous in approaching my drawings now for my patents and the vision I have of the marketing material, or even the way I present myself. I always make sure my living space is clean and well kept, whether I am single or married.

I believe having a clean environment helps you think clearly and makes you coordinated. Applying this type of lifestyle will help your projects, your designs, and your patient care. There is no way you can be disorganized in your personal life and expect to be genuinely organized when dealing with a patient or opening a business. As I heard once, a little OCD goes a long way. A simple trick I have used to help myself become better standardized was that I always looked at things like the next step. I never looked at things as "step 100." I have to do this, and it's 100 steps. I never looked at it like 100 steps. I always looked at it as the next step, and that's what helped organize my approach. Even today, if I walk into my office and my desk is in disarray, I have to clean it up before I even start working. When I leave my office, I love to leave it organized, so I'm ready to work when I walk in the next day. It is imperative to embrace the spirit of organization as you're inventing and becoming an entrepreneur.

You do this by focusing on the first step and then the next step after that. If the next step is obtaining money through a loan, don't look at the 10th step of applying for loans. Get on the website, step one, plug in your name. After you do this part, step two and then step three. Following this thought process was, and still is, the model we use in CathWear. We are always willing to do the next step, whatever it is. A lot of businesses fail because someone didn't want to take the next step. I also would implement a "hot potato" concept within CathWear. We never wanted anyone waiting for us on something needed to move things along. We have a fast turn around time when things are required from us. We would instead be waiting on a potential lead than a potential lead waiting on CathWear.

CHAPTER 3:
LAUNCHING THE RIGHT PRODUCTS

Often we invent ideas in our minds but seldom are they successfully produced. If you haven't established the base or even researched the market for the concept, how will you know if it will be successful? Regularly, people come to me with ideas to get my opinion. The question you have to ask yourself is, *what problem am I solving?* Do people want it, and if so, how bad do they want it? I had someone tell me they wanted to invent a watch that had a pen. You could stick the pen inside the watch, and it kind of retraced and folded on itself into a button.

I just remember thinking to myself, "Why?" Why would I do that when I can have a pen in my pocket? I can have a pen in my scrub top. I can have a pen on my ID badge. I can have a pen on my desk. You know, I didn't know how to tell this person it wasn't a good idea. I also knew this person wasn't going to pursue it. I just had that feeling based on experience from the myriad of people I've met who don't follow their visions. Most people don't patent their ideas because of either a lack of motivation or failing to realize how it will impact patient care. It is critical not to launch just any product, but the right product.

I have other inventions in my mind which I haven't even patented yet. I know there's a need for them because I see the problem remain unsolved in healthcare. I haven't had the time to develop the drawings, apply for a patent, and bring it to market, but I hope I will, at some point. Generally, the inventions which come to you are usually during struggles you are having in your professional career as you are working throughout your day. Someone invited me to a meeting that took place once a month where people would sit around in a dark room and see what ideas would come up. Let's just say that I didn't stay very long, nor did I ever return. I went for a few minutes and couldn't stand to be there for another second. That's not the way to invent something. I have heard people say, "I keep my eye open every day to see if this something I can invent." There is no real gimmick you can implement where ideas magically appear. As the saying goes, *necessity is the mother of all inventions.* We often hear, and quite possibly have said this ourselves, "Why didn't I think of that?" This statement is so popular because they are having the same problem as you are, yet at the same time, they didn't think to do something about it by inventing a solution. It is critical to understand:

- How big is your market?

- Who is your customer?

- Where do they buy?

- How often do they buy?

- When do they buy?

- How many do they buy?

Another thing to consider is how durable your invention is. For example, CathWear's design allows it to last the patient for years like regular underwear. I designed CathWear to be machine washable and durable, as it will replace the patient's regular underwear. It's not very fortunate for CathWear to make a product last this long, yet at the same time, you have to provide a quality product so that the benefits are in favor of the patients and not your pocket. Don't try to come up with the idea that will make you personally successful. It has to be about the patient. So, I built CathWear to be affordable medical underwear designed to help patients who are struggling with wearing leg bags. It's like regular underwear. We have had patients who have been wearing our product going on two years now from our original design. They are still using it today. On paper, it's not very beneficial for CathWear to have built such a great quality product because it keeps patients from coming back and buying more. Still, we're putting out a successful product. I want to encourage you today. Don't try to invent something to become rich, but try and make people's lives better. We can't wait. If you do have a design, you can't wait to be perfect before you launch it. You just have to get it out there, and the market will tell you what needs adjusting if any.

If you launch a product, and after a few years, you're not embarrassed by the way the prototype looks, then you launched too late. Many people have said this. When I launched CathWear, we did a soft launch. I wasn't happy with the design, but I didn't know what needed to be changed and how it needed to be changed until I launched, and I got patient feedback. You can always go back and refine it later. CathWear is on its third version. It keeps evolving, and we keep listening to the patients' feedback. Now, we can make changes and make it better. It's just getting better and better. That's what you can do with your invention. You can get it ready, research the market first, and then patent it. As it goes along, you can always change it. You can always change it and make small adjustments before you do a full launch. I was fortunate enough to know the problem was so severe and unresolved that I just created the medical underwear. I never had an entrepreneurial mind, so I didn't even fathom the thought of researching the market to see if there were other products like it. If you look at all of the competitors' negative reviews, they are all the features and benefits of CathWear. It seems as if someone went and compiled the competitors' negative reviews and built a product in reverse order. The benefits truly highlight the strength of the innovation behind the greatest medical undergarment ever created, called CathWear.

CHAPTER 4:
INVENTIONS AND PROTOTYPES

I believe the second most significant way to invent something is to build a prototype first. Building a prototype gives it a high probability of success and an increased likelihood of obtaining a patent. Think about it. You ask someone to create something for you that you can (or cannot) make yourself. If you can make it yourself at the novice level, it gives hope to the invention when you are presenting either to a team of investors or a company to which you would like to license it. People have ideas, and that's as far as it goes many times. There's a quote that is inspiring to me from Mary Kay:

"Ideas are a dime a dozen. People who implement them are priceless."

The most significant way to invent a product is to create drawings for it first. This way, as you start to draw it, it starts to come to life. Then as you draw it, develop lines like a diagram to explain each feature. As you begin to explain every aspect of the design, you'll uncover more things you can either add or omit. When you do the drawings, make them from different angles, and continue to diagram and explain. It's so fun doing this. I love this stage of the innovation process. I've always had the heart of a teacher, which is how I think I landed at nursing because I get the chance to educate patients on their current healthcare status. You may even realize that your invention has already been invented or isn't that significant of a design. Both of those are great because you are learning your destiny at that moment. It is better to know at this stage that it will not work rather than to open a business and find out the hard way.

An invention is something tangible. Innovation is changing a system. When I say how to invent something, my focus is on an actual invention, a real device. I followed these steps as I designed CathWear and also for the surgical clip I invented. It doesn't have to be a working prototype, in the sense that you can hand it to a patient and they use it, but the concept has to be visible. And again, something tangible.

One of the most critical roles nurses specialize in is educating patients. You have to have on your 'educators hat' during the innovation or invention process. Once the prototype is established, you now have a product to show people. You have to be the catalyst for this portion of the journey. You have to be the one to show people who can help you grow the business. You are the nurse. You are the inventor. You need to showcase your invention and highlight the features. Nobody knows your invention better than you. You have a 'Ph.D.' in your design.

It's vital to research the market before doing this unless you have anecdotal evidence and clinical experience that there is not a solution already made at the time. You need to know what's out there. You have to understand what the nurses are using and what they're not using. If there is some variation of your idea out there, you might want to stop and do some market research. For CathWear, I decided just to press forward. I had no idea what market research was at the time.

1. After you build a prototype and have your drawings, I recommend bringing it to a patent attorney. Once you present it to a patent attorney, he or she is going to want the graphics. The drawings are essential because as you draw them and write down the vision, you are essentially helping yourself understand your design. You will have time to see the flaws in the features and highlight the strengths. You'd be amazed by how clear things will become when you start to draw your invention from different angles and perspectives. They will want to see the prototype, and then you will educate the attorney on how it works. Make sure you get a second opinion by going to two or more different patent attorneys. See what they say and assess what one says versus the other. I wouldn't let either know that you're talking to another attorney because you want to keep it unbiased to get the best information.

2. Next, they'll do a patent search for you. This part is somewhat of a gamble. If you invent something, and there is a patent already out, even if the product was never brought to market, if someone just invented it, patented it, and

threw the invention in the garage, the patent still has an owner. A patent attorney understands this process, and this step develops at this stage. They will do a patent search for the things which are similar to what you have invented.

The process can take one to two years. During this time, don't just sit around and wait. Start trying to improve on the design, make more prototypes, and get patients using your product. It's similar to cooking. When you cook and put a turkey in the oven, it will need to cook for two hours. You don't put the turkey in the oven and then just sit in front of the oven. You're cleaning the dishes, preparing the table, and making the other complementary foods to accompany the turkey. When the meal is done, everything else can now accompany the main dish. While you are waiting on the patent is the best time to start building your team, vision, and parts you control. Understanding this process is why I avoided the impact of setbacks or failures because I could pivot at any moment and realized there was always something else I could be doing to grow the business in another area.

Once the patent is approved, you want to form the company. What type of company do you want? Do you know what an LLC is? Do you want a C Corp? Those are all things you have to decide as you are going along. If you are like I am, many nurses will struggle; you have no business background. All I knew was my business partner, and his girlfriend added a feature to CathWear. We also knew we didn't want to leave the clinical setting. I never wanted to do any bookkeeping; I never wanted to negotiate any deals; I didn't want to deal with an inventory. I didn't want to do any of that. It's essential as you're waiting on the patent process to be finalized to start thinking about what you want to do and don't want to do within the business's development. The best way to build a company is to outsource the things you know you don't want to do.

At this stage of CathWear, I was going through my issues, as I mentioned earlier. I had to put my entire life on hold. I dropped out of nursing school after my second year for two years. I left the CathWear patent on the shelf, and it just sat there. I didn't do anything with it because I needed to navigate the storms in my life; I needed to get my head right. I needed to have my head clear from the personal struggles that were plaguing my life. Once I could get all of this under control and get it all behind me, I went back to nursing school after a 2-year break and graduated top of my class from the University of Massachusetts. I put my entire focus on building the company. I ended up running into a friend from high school who mentioned to me another friend from high school, Edwin Alvarez, who already had his master's degree in business. A symbiotic relationship developed because he wanted to do what I didn't want to do on the business side.

Interestingly enough, he didn't want to do what I wanted to do on the nursing side. He wanted nothing to do with anything medical. We established a perfect scenario for each other because Edwin was the other half of the company. Working with him was the greatest thing that ever happened to me within this venture. I learned so many lessons from him, albeit many of them harsh business lessons. Edwin taught me so much via his natural way of thinking, and I was also able to apply some of it to my personal life.

CHAPTER 5:
ADAPTIVE

If you haven't paid attention to any of the other chapters in this book, then this is the time to tune in. I believe what I will discuss in this section of the book is where you will learn the most and minimize walking into the same emotional pitfalls within a business setting as I did. Nurses are naturally passionate, which is what allows us to provide excellent patient care. Everything we do to care for our patients is not only from evidence-based practice but also "emotionally based practice." Healthcare workers go above and beyond for our patients regardless of what it will take. Character traits like this can cause many complications for an emotional person embarking on an entrepreneurial journey, especially a nurse. The business world is very cut and dry, driven by hard facts, data, and numbers.

Most decisions are made based on the original business plan, and any variation will have to include the entire team. We must not build a team, thinking every decision will be solely based on a nurse's perspective, which may not be the best decision. When starting a business, you have to decide how you will manage the team and business decisions to have a successful future. I decided that there would be no specific person given the task of CEO, and there would be no janitor either when it comes to CathWear. I implemented a policy when I started CathWear, which was: the best decision always wins. At times, we want to apply our ideas, and although this may make sense, it proves to undercut any success before it even starts. Influential leaders let people make decisions within their organization, even if they disagree with the decision, so the entire team is growing. If the decision made by another team member works, then the team member who made the decision grows, and in turn, your team becomes more vigorous. On the other side, If the decision turns out to be a bad one, then the situation can be used as a great teaching moment for everybody to learn, and this will also allow for team growth. If you think you're going to have a successful company by calling all the shots because this is your invention, vision, or innovation, then you might as well just stop now because you will be doomed for failure. At every turn, along with the project, we always went with the best decision which would give us the greatest chance of success, and this formula proved to be extremely successful for CathWear.

As we started to grow, I made one of the worst business decisions I ever made. I went into this project on an emotional high, thinking Edwin and I would be best friends. I never thought it would be strictly a business relationship, even though he made this boundary clear when we formed the company. He said to me at one point, "If it weren't for CathWear, we'd never be talking to each other. I'm not coming into this project, thinking you and I are going to be friends." I underestimated these words, and because of my nursing character, I tend to be more passionate; I believed it was only a matter of time before we were friends. Desiring a friendship, in addition to a business partner, clouded my ability to lead successfully for quite some time, and I had to fight through Edwin's choice of us not being or becoming friends. We work exceptionally well together, and we make all decisions with the company's future in mind. Edwin and I feed off each other positively because we are so opposite from each other. He is entirely the opposite of a nurse, and I believe many business-minded people are just like Edward. We must understand that emotions and business do not mix. Edwin is evident and cut with the way he thinks and runs a business. All of his decisions generate from tangible evidence, and then he makes a very opposite decision from my way of doing things.

Edwin and I have a joke where we always tell people that if the company was left up to me, we would go broke because I give away so many free CathWear units to patients in need. It's the nursing side of me. When I see somebody who needs help, I don't think of the financial implications of giving away free products. The other side of the joke is, we wouldn't sell anything if Edwin were solely running the company because he would charge so much per unit and never help anyone, which would ultimately close the doors. Edwin has a very straight edge character, and I am more loosely fit together. He pulls one way to an extreme, and I pull to the other side to an extreme that we end up going straight up the success ladder. I had to learn to respect our differences in beliefs and life philosophies. There were things that he did not necessarily believe as I did, and I didn't realize I was pushing my views on him, whether it was business-related or in my personal life. We must understand that we have a common goal, which is to grow a successful business, yet at the same time, it may not equate to the growth of a personal friendship or relationship. Most nurses will struggle to control all of the ideas that flow through a company and manage their emotional pulses. It is imperative to understand that nothing can be above the company's goals and trajectory. Somebody may put you in a situation where you are not developing a friendship. Still, you are working exceptionally well together to impact patient care.

It took me three and a half years to realize Edwin meant what he said when he said we were not going to be friends. I recall inviting him to hang out on countless occasions, and 90% of the time, there would be no response to the text message. However, in his defense, every time I asked him a question based on the business, I would get a response immediately. I still didn't see all of this until we got further into the project. I let my emotions get the best of me, and I always felt offended by the rejection of a friendship. Yet, I am surprised at how I could grow a successful company while fighting the reality of none of my business partners or investors becoming my personal friends. The inability to think through this ended up being a massive mistake because I didn't balance my expectations with reality, leading to rejection. This wasn't a rejection of my invitation to become friends. What was happening was me not realizing I was in a different world. Again, this is an area in the entrepreneurial kingdom where I believe many people will fail. I've never been in a situation where I was in a business setting or opening a business. Entering into the business world was all very new and foreign, and I learned how to navigate the journey as I went along. For Edwin, this was normal for him because he thrived in a business setting with the way he was emotionally built. I struggled. I struggled for a long time, and when I finally decided only to contact him when it was business-related, I found peace. I want to discuss this as part of the book because I want the reader to go into their entrepreneurial journey, well-equipped with patient care in mind and not any personal agendas as I did.

Because Edwin and I think so differently, we could make the best decision each time for the company. There were times I had to completely surrender to the way he wanted to do a particular task or decision. There were also times where he had to completely surrender to the way I wanted to run the company, and it was a give-and-take. There was strength in our opposition. I sacrificed every decision to the company because he had made so many consecutive successful decisions that I could completely trust him. When we formed the company, I thought I would have the final say in every company area. We sought legal advice for many things, including a formal contract with all business owners and investors. During this time, the lawyer stated that it was not a good idea to have one person make all decisions. Understanding this change was very difficult for me, but only for a brief moment, because I had the end goal in mind, building an international company for the greatest medical undergarment ever created. I was willing to put my pride aside to reach that goal. I had to figure out what was truly important to me and discard the rest. I decided that I wanted the final say in anything which projected the image of the company. The company's image includes marketing material, captions on posts or advertising paraphernalia, hiring of employees, and anything seen with the visible eye.

I had a vision of what I wanted the company to look like, and I decided that I would be willing to let the rest go if I could have that. For me, this was one of the most excellent business decisions I ever made. Trusting Edwin to handle the rest of the company ultimately was one of the greatest business decisions I ever made. To reach greater heights in the entrepreneurial kingdom, you have to be willing to be flexible, remove pride at every turn, and rise high to impact healthcare to help the patient need your innovations and inventions.

Edwin made some very harsh business decisions, which left me completely in shock, and it was very eye-opening to me that I had stepped into a world where I had no idea what was truly going on. I want to elaborate on precisely what I mean when I say, "harsh business lessons." We had applied for our first business loan of one hundred thousand dollars to jumpstart the company's growth. The upper management team consisted of Hector, Doris, Edwin, and me. To get the loan, everyone had to sign the contract, and Edwin was unwilling to do this. Whoever signed the contract was responsible for the money regardless of what happened to the company, whether it was successful or failed. I never thought that he would not sign this contract in a million years until we had a phone call one night. The entire company was on hold, and I didn't understand how we had gotten to this point because the nurse in me was not thinking like a businessman in him. The way Edwin thinks is to always self-preserve no matter the cost, which is very opposite from me. I put myself in vulnerable positions, and I'm willing to put myself at risk. I explained to him if we all didn't sign the contract, we would lose the loan, and in turn, the project would come to a screeching halt because we didn't have the money to launch.

He replied with little to no concern and only made sure that he wasn't tied to the loan's life so that he and his family would not carry a burden if the company failed. I was blown away and struggled to understand what was happening at this moment. Without a doubt, many people reading this book, who driven by their emotions, will also struggle as well. I will repeat, my goal is to help you navigate the entrepreneurial kingdom to be emotionless when needed and more practical as often as you can. He ended the call with a statement that resonates in my mind until this day. I can hear the words clearly as I'm writing this book because it impacted my life that much. I said, "Are you willing to undercut the project by not signing the loan and stopping everything we've done because you don't want your name tied to this loan for the $100,000?" He responded, "Yes. Let me know if you need anything else from me," then he hung up the phone.

I was left speechless. This conversation was and will always be the coldest and harshest business lesson I ever learned, and even though I understand where Edwin is coming from, it still shocks me every time I think of it. The CathWear team, at this point, were all born and raised into poverty with an opportunity to grow a potentially multi-million dollar a year company. To walk away from a promising intervention with a lucrative market because you have to sign a $100,000 loan shows we are on two different sides of the spectrum.

He ended up signing the loan only because there was a clause in the loan verbiage, which stated each person would be held accountable according to their percentage of the company owned for each monthly payment. Edwin was willing to walk away from this potentially multi-million dollar dream, and I never understood how he came to that conclusion. I struggled with his desire to keep himself in an advantageous position within the company when I've been in a situation where I can't do that. He taught me that this is the reason that I am the CEO, and it carries with it a different burden which he didn't have or want. There's so much more I want to discuss what was running through my mind during this time. I want to keep sharing with you the things which I have learned throughout this journey. Edwin taught me how to be a leader in the business world. He taught me the importance of taking responsibility for CathWear's current status, no matter what situation. He took the time to teach me how to think like a CEO and remove my emotions from making business decisions. I know that I am much more well-balanced now than before I started working with him at CathWear.

We continuously have our differences, and both of our characters and convictions are very strong. Yet, we always meet somewhere between for the company's greater good, and I am forever thankful to Edwin for this. I was perfectly comfortable being the second person in command. I had checked my ego at the door long ago, and I knew that in the areas where I was weak, I was going to have to play second fiddle. He is half of the brain, which I don't have, and I am half of the brain, which he doesn't have. I would never have gotten to this point if I didn't allow myself to be flexible. I learned a new trade of being a CEO and leader of an international and potentially multimillion-dollar company. I regularly put myself last and surrendered the concept of always being right. I decided to slow down my thoughts and emotions and listen to Edwin. His teachings transcended into my personal life, and I started to find success in other areas outside of my business ventures. I hope that I was able to impact his life in some capacity. He is very reserved and keeps everything to himself, so I certainly will never know, but the nurse in me is very open with my feelings and thoughts. I would always try to make sure he knew that I appreciated everything he has done for me in my life.

Edwin was solely responsible for obtaining a Medicare approval code and getting us certified as a veteran and minority-owned company. These three things turned out to be pivotal decisions that he made on his own. The longer we work together, the more we would develop a working silently pattern as individuals and then present the final product during our weekly team meetings. For example, I didn't know that he was getting the

Medicare approval code or the minority and veteran certifications. I found out once he finished completing the steps were completed. Waiting to show the finished work would be the blueprint for our success, as I did the same thing. When I would develop leads with national distributors, I would do the same thing. We felt this was best to maximize our communication efforts and only speak about leads or accomplishments, which were imminent. Edwin taught me early on during our business relationship how to value time. Learning how to value time came via another harsh lesson, and it was also complicated for me to understand. I decided it would be beneficial to establish a weekly phone call to plan for the week and debrief from the week before. On one of the calls, I couldn't have everything I needed for the conference call, and I asked him to give me a few minutes to gather myself.

He told me to call him when I was ready, and I repeated that it would be just a few minutes. He responded, "My time is too valuable. Please call me when you're ready." I said, "You'd rather I hang up and call you back than to wait 3 minutes?" He said, "Yes," and hung up the phone. My experience on this call was something I would apply to every interaction with him going forward. I would make sure that I was ready for each call with the list of things that I was going to speak to him, and although this may sound harsh, I found myself doing it in other areas of my life as well; and so I also learned to value my own time as well. I am transparent about all of these things, not necessarily to speak about my business partner, but to give the reader insight into some of the things you will face when trying to open a business. You have to learn to be flexible and understand where other people are coming from, especially if you are a healthcare worker entering the corporate world.

I always visualized my relationship with Edwin as two military soldiers sitting in a foxhole together. We have to get along to finish the mission, and it didn't matter if we would disagree or often "butt-heads." We knew we couldn't survive one without the other. We averaged one huge argument per calendar quarter because of the intensity of the business venture we were on--not to mention all of the other things we were dealing with within our personal lives. By nature, I apologize when I am wrong, and I do this to grow as an individual. I knew there were only two of us, so there was some involvement on my part, which contributed to any turmoil. I believe in holding oneself accountable. I emphasize this so you will learn to work with people who are opposite of you. You can learn from each other, so you not only open a successful business, but you are also growing as an individual. Edwin and I don't even follow each other on social media or even "like" each other's posts. I have a personal understanding of social media, and it has yet to fail me. If someone doesn't like your posts but is always on social media posting pictures or whatever themselves, then this means they most assuredly don't like you as a person or approve of what you're doing. I have seen, time and time again, people who never support me on social media, and every time I come to find out, they never truly liked me or my projects, per se. Often people have laughed at me when I show them this trait by people on social media, and just as often, they come right back months later and tell me how true this philosophy is. People read this book right now who have seen many of the posts I have made on Linkedin (or other social media platforms) and have never liked my stuff and know what I am saying is true. People don't necessarily disagree or disapprove of what you're doing; It's just that it's you doing it.

I find that to be the oddest thing because I never would've thought it would be like this with him on social media, yet at the same time, this is precisely the way it was supposed to be. Edwin didn't come to CathWear to be my friend. He came to help me with the things I could not do myself, and that's where it stops.

I knew I was invincible with Edwin on the team, and we both could handle any scenario which may present itself to grow CathWear. I would walk into a room, and the intimidation wasn't there anymore. We had already learned how to walk in stride within the project despite our differences. After I would pitch CathWear to a potential client, we would allow time for questions. We both knew what questions belonged to him and which ones belonged to me. It is truly an art and gift to flow with someone like this at such a high level, in a room full of intelligent people with the goal in mind to impact healthcare like never seen before.

Edwin would answer any business-related questions, and I would answer the medical questions. What started to happen is that we began to learn each other's responses, and then we began to branch out. I began to hone in on his answers, and this was explosive because of my weakness. Business jargon became a strength, and he was becoming an honorary nurse, as we often joke. We didn't and still don't have a large team to run this company, and the fact that we are both self-motivated gave us a fighting chance to push through without much of a salesforce. When we designed a business plan, we knew every patient would wear the CathWear unit to their doctor's appointment, and in turn, promote our product. It was as if every patient was a pseudo-sales rep. We constantly had doctors calling us to inquire about our product.

Edwin coming into my life, allowed for a significant shift and propelled me onto the international platform, which I would never have imagined. I believe this is always because of my desire to cheer people on during their endeavors. I enjoyed always clapping for people along their journey. Their accomplishments felt like I was a part of them too. Living my life, rooting for other people's success, was something I believe came back around in life to "water my efforts" and generate growth. I was always commenting on and liking people's posts to encourage what they were doing in their lives because I knew how difficult it is to achieve greatness. I also know that not everyone is going to do the same for me. I know some people are not clapping for me along my journey, and that is perfectly okay because it is none of my business what they do or doesn't do. Edwin felt more to me like an older brother, even though we were the same age. I always had a desire, like a younger brother, to make him proud.

Here are ten steps people often make when starting a business:

1. No plan

2. Spending too much money first

3. Expecting fast results for no effort

4. Hiring too soon

5. Not surveying potential clients.

6. Copying others

7. Not passionate about your business

8. Doing it alone

9. Thinking busy is productive.

10. Not starting today

I believe, and without a doubt in my mind, we never made any of these mistakes. Avoiding these pitfalls was because of how powerful our team was built, and it all started with Edwin.

Our decision-making process was a give and take. We both had choices we each wanted to make. Edwin allowed for the decision making to be fluid and less rigid, at times, as was I with him. He is very analytical and has shown me an excellent track record within the journey. I learned to let go and let it flow. In turn, we grew CathWear onto the international market.

Edwin and I had very different managing styles, and it created quite the balance. My management style is to keep a proactive approach with the company's trajectory, and he has a reactive approach. I would like to anticipate what's coming and plan where and when we could. Not being able to see a trend or data to base his decisions off bothered Edwin because it was the unknown, and as I mentioned, he deals in absolutes. I believe most business-minded people think in this fashion. However, nurses train to watch for patient trends and anticipate what's coming next to provide adequate care for people under our care. I developed this style not only in CathWear but also in my personal life. I tend to walk by faith and not by sight, so this was an easy application. It was hard for me to make many decisions at CathWear because I couldn't "prove" with hard data what I saw coming or not coming. Most of the time, I would willingly surrender to Edwin's management style because it had proven successful, and I wanted him to grow as a leader.

I knew this would mean minimizing myself so Edwin could increase. Plus, it would lead to less bickering back and forth, allowing for a better work environment. I was comfortable with Edwin making the majority of the decisions as I watched and learned. His style was very informative and gave him the hard data he needed to have fewer disagreements and have the problems and situations speak for themselves. He would allow things to "break," and then we could all see a problem that needs fixing. He would allow people to fail with their processes to show them their way of doing it had evidence of not working to the benefit of CathWear.

I struggled with this management style, but I must admit it was very informative and allowed for a clear direction within the decision-making process. I would rather be wrong on what I thought would happen instead of letting someone or a process failure. I believe you have to think about the people on your team and not look to differences as a weakness but instead, as a balance of how you do things. Edwin argued a lot less than I did with his managing style, and there's value in that. I looked at it like, I've come too far to let "my baby" get hurt, and we gotta do something about it. I chose to let it flow, and we made it all work out for the good of impacting healthcare and the lives of the people we were helping. As a nurse, we have to realize that our way of doing things may not work all the time in another professional field. I believe in over-communicating within the team. If you're working on something, then I like to follow-up and get updates and things of the sort. Others didn't work like that, and I struggled in this area as well. People would like to work on a task and then report back when completed. This teamwork style didn't sit well with me because there were times when things would go wrong, and if we would've been talking about all things through each step, we could've prevented it. Other times, it wasn't necessary to speak about it. Everything is balance.

CHAPTER 6:
VISION AND PURPOSE

A man or a woman without a clear vision lives a very loose life. But a person with a vision lives a very narrow and focused life. This perspective of your vision is critical to observe and apply to your own life. Disciplined people live very narrowly. When a man or a woman has a vision, their life becomes very tight. Why? Capturing a vision simplifies your life. When you capture a vision, it simplifies everything because vision controls all of your choices after that. Once you know where you're going, you also automatically know what roads will not take you there. If you know what to do, you automatically know what you shouldn't do. Vision defines your, "what to do" in life. Vision gives you your permanent address, and in turn, it shows you your destination in life. Your destiny dictates your decision. So life becomes simple. If someone offers you something, and it doesn't collaborate in its unity with your vision, then it's easy to say no. Without a vision, it becomes difficult for you to refuse things, so life becomes complicated. The pressure is off, and the focus intensifies. We were not born to do everything. We somehow have this attitude that we have a lot of things to do in life. We don't have a lot to do in life. When you study some of the most influential people, they all have focused on one area of their lives.

Tom Brady focused on football. Michael Jordan focused on basketball. Leonardo Da Vinci focused on the arts. Johnny Depp focused on making movies. Steve Jobs focused on growing his brand and wore the same style of clothes every day. I remember watching an interview with him, and they asked him why he always wears the same outfit. His answer unlocked something within me. He said that wearing the same thing every day eliminated the energy and thought process of picking out an outfit. I started to think about how much time we waste shopping for clothes, matching our outfits, and the time invested in dressing up each day.

I began to do the same thing with my own life, but not to this extreme. I think we can all think of someone like this, who has grown their name and product into an international brand. This thought process helped them all become very influential. You have to get to the point where you are only living for one thing. Your vision will significantly simplify your life in ways which you would have never imagined. This understanding of how the vision will impact your life is beneficial in time management. You will live healthier. There is less stress. Stress comes from not knowing what to do. Your vision will help you create self-discipline as you start to hone in on time required to work on this project. Don't get caught up in being busy and miss the opportunity to be productive. We often fill our schedule with so many random things that don't focus on the end goal, and we think this means we're working hard. Many people who know me in recent years know that I haven't changed. I've grown, but I haven't changed. There is a big difference between growing and changing. I have grown in my knowledge and my experience, but I haven't changed. I have the same intent. Grasping this truth has made my life very simple. I am still the same guy with the same message.

I've been very persistent and remarkably consistent, which are two drastically different things. You can't be everything to everyone. Only a few things are necessary. Only a few things are permissible. Only a few things are beneficial. I don't care how old you are now. You will soon be dead. Seventy years is so short, and you don't have time to make any mistakes anymore. If you are over 40 years old, you are already over the 50% mark. It is imperative to define your vision quickly, as there is no time for experimentation. You cannot allow time to waste any more days. These years of your life is the time for intentional living. You have to know where you're going now. We are too late in life to take detours and cut corners. As you start to finish this book, I challenge you to start thinking about your purpose in life and what your vision will be. Some people in your life are not necessary. Some of you have the wrong company, and they are eating up your time, such as going out to dinner and places with people that aren't directly tied to reaching your goals. "Time Vampires" will hinder where you're supposed to get to because these people will create distractions. Some of the books you've been buying are not necessary; fashion, romance novels, magazines, etc. None of these things help you get to your dream. Your vision will simplify your life because you'll be able to walk up to a bookshelf in a bookstore and know which books not to buy.

We've all heard the statement before: "Jack of all trades, master to none." You become a leader when you find the thing you're supposed to master. Everything that you do is supposed to be motivated by your vision. Vision is supposed to be the source of your human motivation. Vision simplifies your life; I can't repeat it enough. Your vision helps you identify yourself before the people in the world because they know who you are and know what reasons to come to you. Most people find themselves financially struggling, and it's not because they are poverty-stricken, but more so because they don't know who they are or who they were created to be. If you want to be successful, do not seek success. Seek to become a person of value. It is critical to make yourself valuable with the problem that you solve, and the finances will take care of themselves.

Develop a product so dynamic and practical that people will pay for it. Knowing that people are paying me for an invention, which I created and brought to life, is one of the greatest motivators which comes to mind. I used to do all the shipping for the first two years we were open for business. I didn't mind it all because I felt such a massive rush of inspiration and adrenaline as I was packing up units to ship, nationally and internationally. I didn't need reminding to do a particular task because the passion I had for my vision was driving itself. I used to love walking out to the mailbox and leaving loads and loads of CathWear units for the postman to pick up each day. There is no better feeling in the world when you see people buying your product and getting outstanding reviews for all the public to read. I have such a passion for the journey I'm on, and I haven't even gotten my first paycheck--and it's been almost ten years since I first had the vision in the operating room! I work for the love of the journey. I work for the people I speak with who tell me how the product I invented changed their lives or even a family member's life. I field all of the customer service calls, and I have no problem doing this because my vision has is simplified, and I can now sit within these boundaries and excel. I get excited for the patients when they call our website, and they get a live nurse on the phone to help them with their catheter and leg bag management concerns.

When your name comes up in a conversation, what do you think people will associate with your name? If someone had to think about something that reminded them of you, what would that be? Those are serious questions. If they never think about you, that means you have never made yourself valuable, and you have become a "jack of too many trades," and so you've mastered nothing. Become so good in an area that they can't ignore you. Vision is what gives you this unique discovery of what you're supposed to master. All true visions will be tested for authenticity. If your vision is truly going to be successful, life will test it to prove its authenticity. Learn to enjoy environments where your ideas are challenged and are an everyday occurrence. If your product terminates by intense scrutiny, then it was never destined to be great in the first place. You don't have to do tremendous and massive things; you just have to find your vision and master it to the best of your ability.

We're created to do greater things than these and not only to make a living and pay bills. When you discover your vision, it will choose your friends, your library, your use of time, your future, your energy, your life priorities, your hobbies, your diet, your to-do list, your expenses, and how you invest your money. Vision dictates everything, and people who have no vision in their lives, throw off all constraints and have no control for their future. Vision dictates your values because it will dictate how you should behave and what standard you should live your life. Vision clarifies purpose and gives direction to the leader while empowering the leader beyond your assets. Vision does not allow you to live on what you do have but forces you to live on what you don't have. Vision creates resources because people don't give money to people; they give to visions. Your vision will attract resources. Government grants are resources that are looking for visions. When you apply for one of these grants, they don't ask about you, but they ask about the vision you have to determine if they're going to give you the resources. Wise people make decisions that protect their vision. Once you know where you want to go in life, it decides your company. I have very few friends in life, and I don't want them anymore. I have thousands of acquaintances, but I have very few friends. Have friends that will help you reach your goal. Stay away from people that don't want to pursue their dreams because they won't stimulate you and your dreams. Your friends should stimulate your dream because they are supposed to impact you to believe, to keep going, and remain a positive influence. Edwin and I were completely comfortable being the second in command. That's a scarce combination to find when most people are jockeying for the number one position.

I vividly remember when I had reconnected with Edwin. He has a powerful character and presence when he walks into a room, and I have those same characteristics myself. I believe in the power of a hierarchy and the efficiency of establishing a chain of command. I told him, "two lions can live in the same den." I explained to him that the only area where I saw that the project would fail in the long run is if he was unable to realize that this was my vision, and he was being brought on to help me, versus this being his vision and me being brought on to help him. His answer encouraged me, and I know the vision was creating its environment because he immediately said to me, "I had to come to terms with myself that this was your vision, and that I was going to have to tie my trailer to your hitch. I took some time to think about it, and I am comfortable with doing that because I believe we will be successful." This type of decision takes guts. As you start to build your team, you will see how challenging it is to find your vision and someone who has his own and is willing to help you in the process. Your vision will set up all the pieces which you will need for you to be successful. Sometimes you have to leave people behind for you to grow and excel and reach greater heights truly. Stay away from people who post a lot of selfies. They are self-centered and will hinder the project with their egos as the milestones and accolades start to pile up. You have to find a great compliment to your vision. It is a great tool to use on how someone will help or hurt your vision by looking at their last five social media posts. If the previous five social media posts are a bunch of selfies, then you're probably dealing with a very selfish and narcissistic person. People who post a lot of selfies don't have much to offer but only themselves. You want to add value to your vision by bringing in people with visions for their own life. You can tell a lot about a person by looking at their social media feeds.

Be careful of people who post selfies and use many filters to alter their photos, whether it be a selfie or not, because this shows their insecurity level. People who take lots of pictures of themselves to show it to the public are not comfortable with their physical presentation. They will have to alter it with all filters social media feeds provides significantly. They could lose confidence either in you or themselves as the project continues to grow; they may also alter the vision or change the trajectory. Stay away from these types of people if you want to impact healthcare significantly and truly advance your vision. Be very careful for people who like their own posts; this should be self-explanatory.

People who have genuinely simplified their lives don't have time to post many bathroom selfies with altered filters. These personality traits tend to be people-pleasers and seek approval from others to feel a sense of validation. They will eventually hinder the process and not be able to switch their minds to a team mentality. People who are like this are not okay with a perceived lesser role when needed and can't be a versatile piece to the puzzle. You have to choose people who will illuminate the life of the project, and to do this, in addition to many other things, you will have to look at their social media posts. It is such an insight into a person's mind, goals, and values. Social media is the platform where people can portray who they are, but they indeed are. Most people are not transparent in a public setting due to our fear and insecurities of getting to know who they are. I have found that the most transparent someone is, the farther they go in life. Social media has allowed us to create the greatest façade known to man. Social media is the "ESPN Highlights" of someone's life. I certainly understand, and I'm also going to be measured with the same ruler. I'm only speaking from my perspective and what I discern when I look at somebody's social media feed.

You can outgrow your friends. A lot of you don't know how dangerous your company is. If you are the smartest one in your group of friends, it is time to leave the group. If they are always asking you the questions, you may think that's great, but that's bad. You want to be in the company of friends who make you think and who expand you. You want to be around people who you need to ask them questions. People who are not doing anything in life want you to join them. They don't want you to abandon them. There are people that I know, professionally and personally, who are still doing the same thing from when I last saw them. I respect their decision(s) for their own life, but I wanted something different for myself. I tried to evolve through different phases of life. I still see them now on social media, posting pictures in the same bars and nightclubs we used to go to, until I ultimately started my life over, this time with a complete focus to reach all of my professional and personal goals. I can still find them in the same location. Vision chooses your friends. Vision means expecting more of your world than what you see. Vision means that you take more bold steps of faith. Pursuing your vision is an adventure that takes courage. Vision is so critical that it makes you believe in a better world, and it becomes more real.

A strong vision inspires passion. This passion transforms and controls your life, and vision is the source of that discipline that life creates. To have unlimited sight, you have to have vision. Without vision, sight has no hope. Therefore, when you have a vision, you can always live amid the vision with a positive attitude, regardless of what you see or any trouble along the journey.

Whatever makes you angry, you were born to solve. As you learn to apply this, you'll realize it is the number one rule of thumb to become an innovator. I live my life with that statement. My wife and I live by that statement. My wife has applied this rule to her life and has seen significant growth. Often, we think someone else will take care of it or that someone else is going to do it. The reason why it bothers you is that you're the one that is supposed to do it. You are the one that is supposed to create that innovation. You are the one that has been given the passion from within to fulfill this task.

As the vision becomes simplified, it begins to grow. Your vision creates more new opportunities for you to solve. Your vision will start to open more doors for you, which you didn't even anticipate when you started your journey. For example, Oriana Beaudette, the Vice President of the Innovation Advisory Board for the American Nurses Association, called me to invite me to be a member of their board. This phone call and the offer was entirely out of nowhere and very unexpected from what I thought I would hear from her. Essentially, my vision, CathWear, opened up other opportunities for me. Within a few minutes of the phone call, she asked me a question that would open up another door for me in the future. She asked me, "Where do you see yourself in two years?" I spoke about what I believe will happen next in my career, but the important part was that this was the first time I was speaking into the air. Now, I want to be clear, I do not believe in speaking things into existence, and I am a firm believer that it is impossible to do that. However, I am also a firm believer that we can speak about things that are supposed to manifest in our lives, and they will happen. My answer to her question was, "I see myself becoming a keynote speaker, traveling around to different locations, speaking to nurses to inspire them to innovate and overcome any mental or physical obstacles." Once I spoke this into the air, I realized my career aspirations had just opened up many more. I want to help people innovate and grow within their careers to all help more patients--together. Your vision may start very simple in that it may be a conglomerate. Never despise small beginnings.

Every great idea starts small. Allow your imagination to run wild, and you will reach new limits and new heights you would never have imagined. Reduce your life down to one sentence. In other words, you have to identify your gifts and your talents somehow. Summarize them down to one sentence to the point where you know who and what I am. This benefit is what I give to the world. This is me, and this is what they will get from me. People exist to help your project, but they have to find you first. You have to capture this in one sentence.

My father always taught me that if you talk about your dreams, they will become goals. If you never talk about your dreams, then that's all they will ever be, just a dream. Learn to challenge yourself. This way, when someone else does challenge you, it doesn't come across as negativity, but a place where you know you'll excel. I believe the best way to achieve your long-term goals is to set up a series of short-term goals as a guide. Learn to celebrate every short-term goal, and before you know it, you will have surpassed your long-term goal. For example, if you desire to be a scientist (long-term goal), start by getting to math class on time (short-term goal). Don't be afraid to fail. There's more information in failure than there ever is in a triumph or accomplishment. Failure is the fuel to success. I have fallen in so many areas that I have not mentioned in this book, and as I look back, I see that all of those failures were giving me the motivation to smash my dreams and goals today while impacting patients' quality of life.

Your greatest enemy is a distraction. Your greatest distraction is not doing bad things but doing good things. Good things are time vampires if they're not focused on your vision. Vision comes in phases and is fulfilled in stages. Learn from others, but never become them.

CHAPTER 7:
PITCHING IDEAS

One of my favorite strengths is my ability to speak publicly. I didn't realize it would eventually benefit me the way it did as I built CathWear. During my collegiate years, I was always the student who was willing to present the entire PowerPoint. We've all been there, and we've all picked which part of the class assignment we wanted to take. I knew most people struggle with public speaking, and research was never my strength because it would bore me. So I would skip out on the research, but I loved presenting. I know a few people are reading this and can confirm how true this is! I now see how impactful it was going to be later in my life with pitching ideas.

Pitching your idea takes a lot of skill. I always created time to practice my pictures before an event, whether in the car or at home, while completing the house tasks. In front of a mirror, I would listen to my page, look at my facial expressions, and practice pausing while I spoke while smiling during the practice session. I would do several recordings on my phone and then listen to them to identify my areas of strength and weakness, and then make adjustments. This practice will allow you to move away from your slides during an actual pitch and speak freely. You only have 30 seconds to a minute to capture someone's attention. There are many ways to pitch an idea, and it will vary from person to person based on your speaking style and innovation. I firmly believe the best way to present your idea at any level is to use an acronym people use called SPIN: Situation, Problem, Implication, and Need. For CathWear, I have ready a:

1. 30-second elevator pitch

2. Two-minute pitch

3. Five-minute pitch

4. 20-minute pitch

Depending on the situation, I'm always prepared to use one of those styles at any time. When you're making cold calls, you have 20 seconds to tell them all of the intricacies of your design, or you'll lose them. People are so tired of fielding phone calls all day. When they pick up your phone call, and you stutter, there is a delay, or there is any hint you're going to drag on the phone call, you will lose any chance at getting past the gatekeeper, a.k.a. front desk receptionist. So it's imperative to know what it is you want to get out of your pitch.

I'll break down the spin acronym according to how I taught the team to use it at CathWear. You can apply it to your innovation as you see fit.

Situation. A patient with a drain post-procedure has to wear a leg bag.

Problem. The bag slides up and down the leg causing a series of complications. Now there are many problems, but I try to use the best for the situation I'm doing my pitch. For CathWear, the problem I usually mention initially is that the bag slides up and down the leg. When I speak to a nurse, I don't want to say the "bag slides up and down the leg" because I want to talk to the nurse on a nursing level. Nurses use Maslow's hierarchy of needs to prioritize their patient's care. I don't want to talk about the leg bag sliding up and down the leg because it's the least essential complication to the patient. I would say the leg bag could affect patient circulation due to the straps being over-tightened. I would also mention the effect on skin integrity and how the strap causes the skin to break down, which puts the patient at risk of infection. I'm going to capture the attention of the nurse when I use the problems in this order.

If I am speaking to a patient, I talk about the embarrassing moments of not being able to wear a skirt, a dress, or shorts in addition to the constant adjusting of the leg bag and clothing.

Implication. I would move to the next letter in the acronym of SPIN, which is Implication. This step is where I involve the person I am pitching my idea to use their own words to highlight the short and long-term effects of wearing a leg bag. I like to ask questions during this phase. I want the people to know what the patient is experiencing when the bag is sliding up and down their leg. I would ask questions like: "What happens when there's a loss of circulation? Have you ever had a patient need an antibiotic because the straps caused a wound that got infected? Have you ever had a situation where there was blood (or fluid) pool in the lower extremities? Have you ever noticed the straps become unsanitary due to sweat?" Now we all know the answers, but I want the nurse to give me the answer. I want it to come out of their mouths so they can hear the problem with their own words. It helps you highlight the problems which may have become commonplace within healthcare.

I want the patient to tell me things like, "I live in a 90-degree climate area, and I have to wear pants." My question would be, "How does it feel not to be able to wear pants in the warm weather? How does it feel when you can't wear shorts? Do you ever feel embarrassed? "

You want to build the need and set yourself up to provide the solution with your product and fill the 'need.'

Need. Now I am ready to present the features of CathWear as the solution to the implications just stated and create the need. When I pitch CathWear in a contest, I give the situation (Letter S), giving the problem (Letter P). I skip the implications because you're not going to ask an audience in the middle of your pitch about their clinical experience. I follow all of this with a presentation of the need (Letter N). I emphasize all of the features of CathWear and maximize innovative design. I highlight each feature by showing how it removes the problems aforementioned. For example, the patient has a lowered infection rate because the velcro strap isn't sliding around on the skin. The patient is no longer at risk for deep vein thrombosis, or the patient is no longer at risk for decreased circulation. The problem ends up helping you pitch your invention as you fill the need.

You don't want to be lengthy and lose the listener's attention when you're pitching to a crowd, angel investors, an invention contest, or even just on a cold call. I was very fortunate because Edwin works for a healthcare giant. One of his jobs is creating presentations and observing hundreds and maybe even thousands of exhibitions a year.

PowerPoint was his strength, and this gave us the most significant boost to impact a presentation. It is essential to leave enough opportunity to engage them afterward. It is crucial to talk about the team and the expertise they bring to the table, including the impact of the design and the profit margins.

When we pitch our ideas, we are prone to be so excited and passionate that it can lead to over-speaking and lose our audience. PowerPoints tend to be very wordy. I hate a wordy PowerPoint. It is always better to have them look at you and keep the slides with just a few pointers because you want to be the pitch's attention and not have people reading your slides and losing the momentum. Always be excited when you're talking about your company, inventions, or innovations. Before you can make people believe in your product, you have to believe yourself. You're the inventor. You are the nurse. You're the medical person personnel. You're the expert. It doesn't matter if someone in the crowd has ten PhDs and has found the cure for cancer. When it comes to your invention, you have a Ph.D. Nobody else knows your product better than you. It doesn't matter who you are pitching it to; you are the expert when you walk into the room. Your confidence has to be at an all-time high because you know your product, and this is precisely how it is in the pitching game as well. I find it extremely critical what you're wearing in the background of a virtual presentation. You don't want to give anybody any reason to discredit you and what you're doing. I've seen many great products pitched by somebody in a T-shirt, and as soon as I saw it, the person completely lost my motivation to listen to them. Now for you, it could be different. I am of the school of thought that I will leave no stone unturned if I dress the best that I can. I don't want to give anyone a reason to walk away from my product and my ideas, and in turn, forsake their patients. I always presented myself in a suit and tie, which was tied correctly and matching. I also made sure I had a professional background and not a picture of my kitchen or family photos in the environment.

Smile as you share a testimony of a patient experience with your product. You can get as creative as you want. Your pitches are your own. As you move along into different inventions, and as your company starts to grow, people will want to know the business plan, distribution channels, customer demographic to include marketing strategy, and things of the sort. You also want to save those for private conversations later on down the line.

- You don't want to have more than ten slides.

- You don't want ever to use a video.

You want to be creative when you're animating the slides in the middle of a pitch. Try not to animate your slides in such an elegant way that it distracts from the pitch but provides more of an easy transition from slide to slide. If you want to ruin your pitch, throw a video in it. It ultimately trips up the momentum. I honestly don't believe when doing a pitch contest that you should ever have a pre-recorded pitch. It shows a lack of preparation, self-confidence and depreciates your ability to lead; it's cowardly. You want to remain the focus of the pitch. You want to get into the pitch, and you want to get out. Your energy counts! People do not want to buy anything from anyone they feel is not showing confidence during the pitch. Never end your pitch by saying, "Thank you."

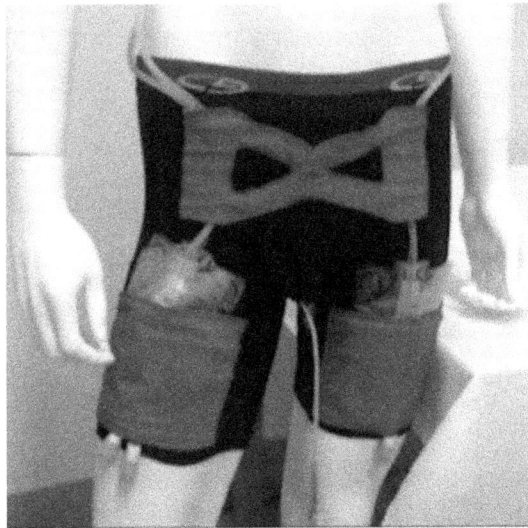

Be creative and end it with an open-ended closing, which will lead you into the Q & A.

At the time of this writing, we have won every contest we've entered. However, towards the end of writing this book, we did have some humbling moments within our journey. We were in the Merrimack Valley Sandbox, which is north of Boston, Massachusetts. It was our first invention contest since we were awarded the patent in

2013. We were made aware of this contest two weeks before the pitch date. After presenting Sandbox with our patented design, we could be a late entrance into the competition. Up to this point, we had never pitched our idea before. When we arrived and set up our booth, the attention was immediately on us because I brought in a six-foot five-inch tall chalk-white manikin. I had a vision of dressing up the manikin as a patient because I wanted to educate any viewer on what we see in the operating room. I believe visuals speak for themselves. I tried to minimize talking by providing a visual, capturing their attention, and then engaging in conversation. This invention contest was right in our hometown, and it was an excellent opportunity to launch the most extraordinary innovation the medical undergarment industry has ever seen. However, I didn't know that you could not read from a piece of paper in your hand when pitching your idea because this was the first time doing something like this via PowerPoint presentation.

When we got up to the stage and set up the manikin, we could hear people in the crowd making joyous sounds as the manikin was capturing their attention. We ended up winning first place and fan favorite. One of the judges mentioned me reading from a piece of paper and then quickly stated that someone informed him that we were a late entry into the contest, so we didn't end up losing points. I learned a valuable lesson, which was the only time I ever pitched with reading from a piece of paper. We got a standing ovation for CathWear. One of the judges gave us his vote, mentioning he had a catheter 20 years ago, and he was surprised there was nothing else like it on the market in 20 years. Someone designed a product to manage the leg bags, and it's also the most recent innovation in the 1960s. Our job was to make those straps obsolete. The prize was $1,000 for first place and $500 for the fan-favorite. I can't recall at the moment exactly what we did with the money. Still, I just remember the feeling of winning and watching myself move onto this inventor stage, possibly at the entrepreneurial level, and it was an extraordinary time.

I wasn't a nurse, yet at this time, but I was in my freshman year in nursing school. I had my radiology degree when we won the contest. We met a lot of people, including lawyers. We had lawyers standing in line, waiting to speak to us. It was a genuinely inspiring experience because it made me believe what I was doing was going to impact the patient's life significantly. I am very thankful for one of the attorneys that we met there because he's the one who told us to bring CathWear to market, and we ended up following his advice years later.

The second invention contest we won was the Massachusetts Innovation Nights. We won first place and another standing ovation. There were booths all around the perimeter in a flea market expo-style. People always flock towards us when we set up our booth because of the visual presentation. Do not underestimate the power of a great visual explanation. Desire to be different and break the mold from the patterns set by inventors and innovators before you. Aspire to leave your mark so others will be able to use it as a template for their business ventures. When we present CathWear, we would always show two manikins, a chalk-white female and a chalk-white male manikin. At times, we would add a third manikin, a child, to highlight the pediatric version for which we were trying to establish the market. CathWear always stole the show no matter where we went, and this speaks to the market and how under-served it was. I wanted to present CathWear in a particular way where it screamed the potential of a multi-million dollar idea.

I would put a biliary drain, gauze with tape and a proper dressing, nephrostomy tubes, a super pubic tube, and a Foley, so as people walked by, it would catch their attention. I wanted the practicality of the features to be visible. So again, as you start to prepare for your invention competitions, you have to get your pitch down into your memory in a series of different pitch styles. You also have to present your prototype for your visual presentation, which is why I had mentioned the importance of having a prototype, even if it's not a working prototype.

The third contest we won was the Hofstra Veterans Venture Challenge out of Long Island, NY. This contest was for $50,000 and used the money to launch an aggressive marketing campaign to propel CathWear into the international market further. This business competition was more of an accelerator, and it was very challenging for me. While becoming a nurse entrepreneur, I was also working full time as a registered nurse. I could not break away from my full-time job to dedicate all of the time required to CathWear, and I also didn't feel I needed to. I was able to do most of my duties as the CEO remotely, attributed to LinkedIn and the career field within nursing I chose, which was for the Visiting Nurses Association (VNA). Working as a visiting nurse allowed me to have access to my phone as I needed it, and I was able to send emails, text messages, and make phone calls on the fly.

There were many virtual conferences I was able to join during COVID-19, and at other times because of the flexibility my schedule allowed. Somebody told us this was just a hobby if one of us wasn't working full time during this program. I do understand in the business world what this means, yet at the same time, I completely disagreed with it because of the current role I had within nursing. I believe a nurse's impression is that we are always by the bedside for eight hours within the four walls, and how could you possibly run a business from this type of environment? This scenario certainly was not the case for me, as I believe I could do both and maximize my time evenly. The impression given was something I was not willing to accept. Because I was working so hard at growing the company, I didn't allow somebody's opinion of how much time I was investing to be determined as me working full time or not. I would often forsake my patient charts being completed at my job to focus on shipping orders, developing leads, virtual in services, and physically cold-calling potential leads.

I was even reprimanded at my job on two occasions because I was falling back in my duties. I highly encourage the person reading this book to fight through any advice given to you from a paradigm set by people who don't understand your ability to have a balanced approach to growing your brand.

The type of job you have will certainly make or break your ability to do both, but it did not break me. This accelerator program was very involved, and because I was on the road, I met all requirements. Edwin had a job where he could not break away, and the only way for us to be successful within this program was if I took it on full-time. Completing this program was an excellent experience for me because my weakness was in business knowledge and understanding. I'm very thankful for Edwin's help because he nearly did every assignment for me, and then I would submit it. Let me elaborate on that part in-depth to understand the importance of working as a team despite personal differences or lack of a friendship.

For every assignment I needed, I would do the parts of the project I could do on my own, and I did it to the best of my ability. Once I finished everything to the best of my knowledge, I would present it to Edwin and add the assignment's missing portion(s). He would return it to me within hours, so I was ready for the next day of the accelerator program. For every PowerPoint slide deck, he would take the grading rubric and set up the entire slide deck because he had to prepare presentations and slide decks frequently, which was a strength of his, and in turn, a strength of the company.

The director of this program recently had a prostatectomy and wore a leg bag similar to the same situation with the previous contest's judge. I share this information because both the judge and the director of the Hofstra competition share this publicly. Since we started this company, we would continuously run into potential business leads and people who would open the door for us in another area. They happened to be wearing a leg bag themselves. We obtained the business loan for one hundred thousand dollars with a man who also had a surgical procedure that required a leg bag. The meeting we had with this gentleman was very motivating to experience. The project started to show us how much of a dire need these patients had and a great solution found in our invention. I learned many valuable lessons from Edwin, and one of the ones that benefited me the most was not celebrating too long after a victory but remaining even-keeled.

I did explain to Edwin a personal observation I have had from my life, and I found it to be true repeatedly. "Every quality you have works for you and against you." Let me explain. If you are a nice person, then everybody invites you to their party. However, since you are a nice person, people will take advantage of you. On the other side, if you are a mean person, nobody will invite you to their party; but no one will be taking advantage of you either. This example is the best analogy I can give for that quote, which I live by, and I have seen it proved repeatedly. The way you are strong in one area will hurt you in another. It's not that I didn't find joy in celebrating small milestones along the way. What I learned was not getting overly excited and letting my emotions override the long journey ahead.

This way of celebrating accomplishments, or any type of progress, was also an area where Edwin and I differed. I learned to celebrate different stages of the many successes and my business ventures with my wife, Eunice, and my children. I do believe being well-balanced in anything and everything in life will get you extremely far. I also know that every quality you have works for you and against you. I think it would be healthy for Edwin to have celebrated more milestones, but that's none of my concern. My focus was on making sure I wasn't over-celebrating and was growing as a person. The victory for Hofstra, in my mind, was very short-lived as I knew $50,000 was certainly not a lot of money for the goal we were trying to reach, yet at the same time, it was everything we needed, and I was very grateful.

Every time we made the newspaper or a magazine interview and even once made the cover of a magazine, I made sure to have a professional plaque made of it to hang on the wall in our office and home. I believe in celebrating small milestones. I believe being self-motivated is something that you can't teach someone. Celebrating the small accomplishments was how I maintained my motivation to continue to push myself into becoming the best CEO and nurse entrepreneur I could be—winning the Hofstra Veterans Challenge during the height of the COVID-19 pandemic. This pandemic was one of the most fantastic times in my life because I learned how to fight through a global shutdown and watched my company increase in sales while so many other companies were closing the doors. The elective surgeries shut down, and these procedures are when drains are placed. We saw financial growth via online sales during the COVID-19 shutdown, which indicated our success trajectory.

The fourth contest was the MassChallenge, which was for one hundred thousand dollars, and this was the most extensive business accelerator competition in New England. I was extremely confident in our ability to win this competition to the point where I was already calculating what we were going to do with the finances, which was to bring on Edwin full time as the COO of CathWear and maximize every possibility to grow the company. When I would pitch CathWear, I would always mention the ability to lower infection rates due to the reduction of skin irritation and the disconnecting of the catheter to the leg bag to change it to the night bag. I would also mention lowering the patient's risk of getting a deep vein thrombosis (DVT) due to the patient not over-tightening the straps to keep the leg bag in place. We didn't have any clinical data from a trial to support this claim besides anecdotal evidence based on my clinical experience. We also didn't have the finances to perform the clinical trial, although we kept an ear open to any possible grants to have this implemented. Are you willing to do whatever it takes for your inventions and innovations to succeed and impact healthcare?

Everyone at this business accelerator was very excited about our invention and groundbreaking design to include every judge and mentor. We advanced past each round until we got to the final round, and we were dismissed from the competition. Every judge gave us very high scores and extraordinary remarks, yet at the same time, they didn't advance us. They suggested we have a clinical trial performed to back up the claims we were making, such as skin irritation, lowering infection rates, and decreasing DVTs' risk (Deep Vein Thrombosis). The early dismissal was very difficult to experience because I had the money spent in my mind, and I learned a valuable lesson on how to remain even-keeled. This situation is an excellent example of why Edwin would always say that he considers it not ours until the money is in the bank account. I just had so much faith to the point where it blinded and humbled me. I had a tough day, and I learned a valuable business and life lesson never to assume anything until completion.

By the end of the day, I was smiling at this humbling lesson I had just learned. This lesson is when my quote, "every quality you have works for you and against you," brought me back to reality. Getting knocked out before the final round was when I knew Edwin had a healthier quality than I did of being even-keeled. I didn't understand why we got dropped from the program for not having the clinical data since the business competition proceeds would've allowed us to pay for it and reach more patients. The fact that the judges gave us such great feedback is what made it more complicated to understand.

The same day we found this out, we received an email from Ohio State University stating they had a program that would help us conduct a clinical program. Something unique always has happened to us during this journey. There was still an open door with each closed door, and it was one of the most motivating feelings I have ever experienced because It gave me hope that we were going to be successful. The next day we were on the phone with Ohio State University getting the initial conversations to have our first clinical trial. I had access to Ohio State University because they invited me to be a speaker at the school to speak with their Master's Degree in Innovation Program in nursing. Edwin gave me the idea to reach out to them a few weeks before dropping from the competition and asking about any possible clinical trial programs.

Here is another example of removing pride from your journey. I know what I don't know, and I am comfortable not knowing what I don't know because it will only be a matter of time before it becomes a strength. I certainly won't quit learning--ever. I decided to make a post on Linkedin and ask for help in obtaining a clinical trial. The following is my exact post:

"Can anyone help me find a way to conduct a clinical trial for CathWear?

I'm flexible with the desired outcomes and willing to learn which ones are the best to keep the focus. I would like to know how much of an impact on patient quality of life. CathWear needs a large sample size for this research. We want to explore the effects of reducing infection rate, pain, hematuria, deep vein thrombosis, skin irritations, and cost-effectiveness while wearing a urinary leg bag.

The target population is Urology patients with bladder cancer. If there are any schools available where students can benefit from the clinical trial, that would be great.

CathWear is registered with the FDA as a Class I Medical Device if anyone needs to know.

Thank you in advance!"

I have no problems putting something like this on a professional platform with millions of smarter people than I am. I have passed the stage of "Imposter Syndrome," and I know how to fight through my weakness to achieve my final goals. This post was such a great decision! I didn't think anyone would respond. It was one of the posts I made this year on LinkedIn, which generated the most traction. I was nervous at first, but I did it anyway. We must learn to gravitate towards fear and the things which scare us the most. Many people commented on the post. The comments allowed the post to circulate more, making it visible within the social media feed for the day. We developed a lead from Stanford University and Massachusetts General Hospital, one of the top hospitals in this magnificent country, for years on end.

I explained the resources available for us at this time to get the clinical trial done and asked if there were any grant programs or US Veteran discounts. Both places assured me my finances would be approved through specific programs to help us accomplish this clinical trial. As I mentioned early in the book, you don't need money to start a business. You need determination and passion for solving a problem, and the money will show up on its own. Your passion will open more doors for you than a job ever will. Your job is what pays you, but your work drives your passion and brings out what you were born to do. It is how momentum builds within your projects, which a business plan simply cannot do or predict. There is a hunger inside of every person who wants to succeed, and this hunger will bring opportunities like the ones I have experienced repeatedly throughout my career.

What happened next is that MGH had just started a partnership program with NIH (National Institutes of Health), and they wanted to showcase CathWear as one of their first companies to start the program. The nurse at MGH said, "I think this would be a great fit for the NIH program we're trying to develop." It all manifested itself because I was willing to put my own needs and any possible self-embarrassment secondary to helping the people in our target market.

I honestly believe that the nurse at MGH and I work so well that it seemed we were always steps ahead along with every phase of the journey. We will reapply next year in 2021 with the clinical data in hand and give it another try. Now that I know what they are looking for as far as information, I will be sure to add it to my pitch to highlight the sophistication of the growth of CathWear. There were so many moments similar to this situation, not only in my own life but also in this journey, which I could use as a growth moment and benefit me later.

The fifth business competition I want to mention is the New York Business Challenge. We won second place and ten thousand dollars. I remember starting to feel extremely humbled after not making it to the Mass Challenge's final round and then coming in second place here. My favorite part about coming in second place at this business competition was the phone call I placed to Edwin afterward to thank him for his efforts, which got us into the contest. We both love to win so much, and we are so competitive that the frustration of not coming in the first place was palpable on the call; yet at the same time, neither of us mentioned anything about not taking first place. The call lasted about 30 seconds, and when I hung up the call, I had a grin on my face because I knew that I had paired up with a natural-born winner.

The sixth competition I will gladly mention is the New England Innovations contest, in which we won first place in our category. This contest did not have any monetary value, but the publicity associated with this event was noteworthy. I am always eager to engage in something that will provide free marketing for our company's growth.

A closed-door still is as powerful as an open door because both give direction. People struggle with getting a "no" for an answer, but I believe a "no" is just as powerful as a "yes." Again, both give a clear direction to the next steps.

CHAPTER 8:
BUILDING A TEAM

I did not know how to build a team. I had never been in a situation outside of playground sports where I had to assemble a team to work on this kind of project. It is critical to identify, write down, and prepare yourself for the vision you have for your team. There are roles within a company that I knew I did not want to do. I didn't want to manage any books. I didn't want to do business stuff like negotiations. Those things simply did not interest me at all. My vision was to remain on the clinical side of this project. So, I identified my weaknesses right there, and now I was able to find someone who was business-minded and liked doing these types of tasks. We must learn to hire our weaknesses, which are someone's strengths. In these types of scenarios, I believe that a lot of nurses and healthcare workers may struggle. You are going to have to learn to be flexible in this area. Most people, by nature, don't want to release control during this process. They don't want to break because naturally, we want to be in control of everything.

As we built our team, we ended up building with Edwin as the first building block. He was our first team member, and he's the one who formed the LLC. He found an attorney and worked on building the contract, the structure, and identifying everyone's position, title, and role. Along the way, things had started to change. Hector ended up moving away and had become almost obsolete. You can't expect other people to have the same motivation level as you or have the same endurance towards the end-goals. As we started building the company, and we started working, Hector began to do a lot less, and I had to continue without him to continue building the dream--at least my dream. In the negotiation process, I had to surrender a part of the company in an area I wanted to have full control, which was to have full control of the company with the final say in any decision. I wanted to be in charge of everything. I didn't want anybody to interfere with the vision I had.

This desire to have this much control can present many complications when forming a company. It becomes a sole proprietorship when a business typically requires less paperwork and is easier to maintain than partnerships or corporations. The business owner is responsible for the debts and liabilities, and the accounting and record-keeping methods are usually simple and straightforward. Unlike a sole proprietorship, an LLC is a hybrid of the partnership and corporate forms that allow the liability protection with the tax advantages of a partnership. I couldn't do it this way, as it didn't give us the best chance to succeed.

We ended up partnering up with almost a handful of private investors, and the investors were people we knew. Three of the investors were personal friends of Edwin and his family. One investor is also a childhood friend of ours and a pastor at a local church. We wanted to work with investors who offered more than just capital. We wanted investors who added value and could do other things to help us grow in the background. As an example, one of the investors worked as an international IT guy, and because of this, he was able to help us build a website and get our company email established. It was free. He was also a carpenter. Somebody gave us free office space, and he volunteered his time to completely renovate it and give us a state-of-the-art contemporary presentation of the office's design.

Another investor had a very high position in Amazon. He was briefly able to educate us on the process of getting onto Amazon, the features of Amazon, and the ins and outs of Amazon in general. We now have the Amazon badge, and we are one of the top sellers on Amazon in our category. Although not directly tied to what this investor brought to the table, it was worth mentioning.

The third investor is a developer of real estate within the community where we all grew up. He buys a lot of property and flips houses. He gave us an office for no money down and

100% rent-free. He was the investor who has the most considerable financial contribution to CathWear, and I stopped by his office one day to thank him for investing in my vision. He said to me, "I didn't invest in the vision you have or the invention you're marketing. I invested in you, Brian, because I believe you are an inspiration to many people, and you are a beacon of light in our community." I was left speechless as my eyes were watering up. Anyone who knows me knows that I am a cry baby. I wear my emotions on my sleeve. I am comfortable being in tune with my feelings in public. I believe it makes me a well-rounded person and increases my confidence. I believe in versatility. I'm honored to have had those words spoken by this one investor because I shared the same sentiment for him. His mother was there for my family when we were younger, and I will never forget what she did for me directly. Having a business relationship with her son is why I feel honored to grow an international business within the community where I was born and raised.

The last investor was a key person at the start of the launch of CathWear because he was young--a millennial who buys everything online. It was great because he had the experience of online shopping via websites such as Amazon. At this stage of CathWear, I was not very keen on buying online because I'm from a different generation where I still believe in people's interactions and cash purchases. Online shopping has changed dramatically in the past year as I find myself busier and busier and purchasing things I need online. This particular investor could fine-tune certain website areas based on what online consumers would be looking more inclined to see. So, here's another investor who took time out of his day, not only to invest his own money into CathWear, but he also became part of the staff.

One of these investors was on our weekly calls, in a daily text thread and helped us make decisions for about a year and a half. I compensated him for all of his time. I gave him two extra percentages on top of what he purchased to pay him for what he did. You must never allow someone to work for free. It's not just because of the implications that could happen later on if things don't go as planned, but if your company expands, someone could come and say, "Oh, I did all this stuff for you," and then bring litigation to you. Everyone should always get compensation for what they do when they are doing anything to help your business. It is easy to think everyone is willing to help you for free, and this may be the case, but when success starts rolling in, people will often change how they feel. I believe this investor would have worked for free because he believed in the vision, yet at the same time, I have to stick to my own beliefs, which are never to let anyone work for free.

One thing I want to mention here is the importance of knowing the difference between negativity and critique. I was willing to work in an environment where the critique of any process was welcomed, but I would not harbor an environment with negativity. I believe that if you don't like the way something is done, and you do not have a better solution on how it could be better accomplished, then I think the person should wait until they have a better way of doing it, or else it will come across as negativity. I was advised people in a project have a job to critique all processes and not implement their solutions. Yet, at the same time, this is not the type of person I was, and it came across as negativity, and I had to remove any negativity, not only in my life but also within CathWear. You have to part ways with negativity and let the chips fall where they may. When the negativity increases, this indicates that their time in the project has come to an end.

I want to add something here, which is critical to understand. When you're a nurse, you tend to talk about the things which "feel good" about the project. Investors don't care about this stuff. We have had so many meetings with them, and in every session, I learned this to be so true. It makes perfect sense, they loaned you their money, and they want to know when they will return on their investment. They don't want to know about the patient who called you crying to say thank you or how many distribution deals you've started. The investors want to know the risks and the way the money is invested. In our last meeting in November 2020, I spoke for about 20 minutes about everything we were working on, including the pediatric version's development. The next day, I called one of the investors who made an interesting comment about knowing the risks as his point of interest. I've known this investor since we were kids, and he was very respectful and extremely professional. He stated that he cared nothing for what I was saying for the 20 minutes I was speaking. I felt so at peace. I think we complicate things in life and within our projects. I could've saved myself so much time on more productive things. I learned, and that's all you can do when working on your dreams--learn. Before the next investor meeting, I will send out an email asking them what questions they have. When we get on the call, I will only gear towards answering those questions and nothing more. If they don't ask a question, there will not be any unnecessary speaking, at least on my behalf. If they don't respond to the email, I will know they didn't need any updates. Do you see how simple things become when we are willing to remove our emotions and balance our growing expectations?

We hired a director of marketing who specializes in Amazon. He is not an investor but brought to the table extreme value. It almost didn't end up this way, as the original negotiations didn't go through. He was asking for more than we were willing to give, and we didn't think his offer was proper for what he brought to the table at the time. We were glad to walk away from any deal which didn't benefit us much, and this was the confidence we had in what we were doing. You have to know that giving up pieces of your young company could cost you more than what you anticipated later on down the road, and we didn't want that to happen to us. After some time had passed, we ended up going back to the negotiation table. We presented him with the same offer we had ended the negotiations with and decided to partner together. Since then, he has given us an entirely new website and has completely optimized our Amazon presence to have a trajectory to be number one in our category.

I feel proud to say that I've always invested in the community in which I grew up. I believe in giving back and taking people with you on journeys such as this. You can inspire the world, but if you don't help grow the people around you, then you've not done much, which will leave a lasting impression. I live by this quote that I came up with on my own, and it's become my mantra:

"Success is better achieved as a community" --Brian O. Mohika

Here is what our team has accomplished: We have a 4.5-star rating and a 5.0-star rating on Google, respectively, with just over a year of launching on Amazon with over 100 reviews. We have reviews from doctors, nurses, caregivers, and most importantly, the patients themselves. I have always said that if you have a bad product, Amazon has a great way of letting you know because reviews are very unforgiving. And I also say the opposite. If you have a good product, the Amazon reviews have a great way of letting you know. The patients have spoken, and their voices have value, whether you have a good or bad invention.

I wasn't going to have everything I wanted while building a brand. I also didn't want a dictatorship with the mentality of, "I'm the boss, everything has to come through me, and I have the final say." I decided what I wanted was to control the image of the company. I tried to control what people see. Anything people can see with the human eyes regarding CathWear in public; I have complete control of it. Marketing, social media posts, the website, and hiring of employees are some of the things which fall into that category. I was allowed financial decisions under or around $2,500, and I could decide without running it by the board. I now had to make company decisions by a vote on a board, and this allowed a lot of safety for me as a business owner and person. It got harder because Hector left. Hector was my partner up to this point, and all of the choices made were between him and me. Now I am in a new business relationship which is very formal. The decision ended up being pivotal for me because I wanted to present CathWear as a Christian-based company that I would dedicate to the Lord. I tried to maintain that image throughout. As I mentioned earlier, I went through some dark times, which led me to encounter Jesus Christ in my living room vision. I remember being depressed, and when God revealed to me He died for my sins and provided the only way into the Kingdom of Heaven as a free gift, I wanted to show God honor.

I think a lot of times, nurses will fail because we have the mentality of the three nurses I mentioned. We tend to want things to be our way usually, or no other way would work. As you build a team, you have to continually remind yourself to remove pride and ego out of the way. I implemented a company policy that the best idea always wins. Everybody would throw their thoughts on the table, and the best idea was the one we went decided to choose. Wanting everything your way hinders growth, momentum, and trajectory.

There is no CEO at CathWear. Everybody is equal. I believe in building a team so strong no one can point out the leader. Everybody does what everybody feels is best as a group. Yes, I didn't necessarily want to do certain things, but I learned how to lead with a surrendering spirit. It was something I honestly learned on my own because nobody taught this to me. When you build a business, you have to remove pride by keeping people in front of you. When you want to go high up the success ladder, you have to adjust to the team's needs and, at times, forsake your desires. I needed to understand the group's personalities better. The same also happened to the team, and they had to adjust to my character. The same way they were teaching me things on business, I had to teach them medical ethics, etiquette, terminology, medical practices, and patient care. I needed to know the importance of putting the patient first because business people don't see the patient care side. Business-minded people see numbers, and that's usually it. Nurses see patient care, and nurses don't see the numbers. You need both of those entities inside a successful group, and we all had to adjust to one another.

I'm the biggest cheerleader at CathWear. Every team needs one person who is the encourager. I didn't want to only focus on the numbers. I tried to focus on the little victories. It didn't matter what situation we found ourselves in, I always saw the positive side, and I never allowed anyone's pessimistic or negative thought pattern to penetrate my ability to see the vision coming to fruition successfully. We faced many setbacks and let downs along this process. Because of balancing my emotions and my naturally positive attitude, I was always able to keep the team uplifted. When we get calls from patients saying we were impacting their lives, I wanted to highlight this to the team. It's essential, and I've said it repeatedly that you have to be the catalyst. I can't emphasize this enough. You can not expect pats on the back. You cannot expect someone to come and pick you up and help you finish the lap. Sometimes you are going to have to crawl, but you're going to get there. It's a balance, and this is one of the most incredible things I learned from Edwin. I would get very excited at the slightest accomplishments, and he wouldn't. I didn't understand why he wasn't as enthusiastic as I was, but now it makes sense. We were supposed to be hitting these milestones, so it shouldn't come as a surprise that needs celebration. Having a balance in any area of your life is always a good thing. Everyone associated with CathWear is from our hometown (Lawrence, MA), whether it is a private investor, vendor, or hired employee.

CHAPTER 9:
USING LINKEDIN TO BUILD YOUR BUSINESS

We launched on Amazon at the end of September 2019. Right at the launch was around the time I got on LinkedIn. LinkedIn would prove to be one of the most excellent marketing decisions I made for CathWear as an individual business owner.

We had a deal we were trying to broker through with Medline during 2018 and 2019. This lead started to develop when I met a registered nurse at a nurse Shark Tank at Northeastern University in Boston, MA. She was the Chief Nursing Officer for Medline. When I met her, she was blown away by CathWear and thought it would be an excellent Medline fit. Once I noticed the deal with Medline started to grow cold, I wanted to reach back to her, not realizing she was no longer at Medline. I decided to search Google for her name. When I did, her name showed a LinkedIn profile, which had popped up. I had set up a LinkedIn account sometime before this—when we first won the Merrimack Valley Sandbox in 2013. Somebody had recommended it. I thought LinkedIn was for people who were looking for employment. I didn't realize it was a place where professionals gathered like a professional Facebook.

Two months before this, I happened to Google my name and saw my LinkedIn profile. I went into my profile and updated everything I possibly could. I did this because I saw things were out of order with something associated with my name, and this all plays into having a clean and organized living environment. There were so many things wrong with my profile! These small adjustments are why I always say a little OCD goes a long way. There were so many outdated things. We used to be called "Drainage Partner" — an impromptu name we picked when we were in the Merrimack Valley Sandbox. I had no profile photo, and nothing was updated. I took my time, went through it with a fine-tooth comb, and set up a professional profile. Now, I'm prepared to reach out to this person.

As I reached out to her, I realized that I started seeing other nurse innovators, entrepreneurs, and leaders. I saw so many nurses with PhDs and unique job descriptions.

I had no idea there were even other nurses inventing stuff to the magnitude that I saw on LinkedIn. The best way to describe it was that I was a big fish in a little pond until I got into LinkedIn. When I joined LinkedIn, I became a small fish in a big pond, which is the best way. *If you're the smartest person in the room, you're in the wrong room*. Well, I certainly wasn't the most intelligent person in the room on LinkedIn. And that's where I want to be. I didn't realize there was much to do for nurses outside of a hospital setting. It never occurred to me the possibility of becoming a nurse entrepreneur, and completely blown away at how many nurse entrepreneurs I have met on LinkedIn. The experience allowed me to thrive as an individual, a business owner, and a builder of the greatest medical undergarment the healthcare industry has ever seen. Once I got on LinkedIn, this consumed all of my time because I was finally able to directly connect with medical personnel in the urology market and focus all of my efforts. I was never one to watch television outside of football and the NBA playoffs. It always puzzled me to hear of people who would sit in front of a television for countless hours watching television shows, shows within a series, Netflix, or things of the sort instead of building their dream. I used to see numerous Facebook posts talking about upcoming shows or specific events that happened to a televised show's character, and I always thought to myself how I didn't have time for that. I always wondered how somebody could utilize their time doing something so meaningless. I can't picture success and a television show combined with one's journey of entrepreneurship.

If you're going to be a successful business owner, you will have to learn to shut the television off and add value to your time by being productive towards your goals. You have to make time for your dreams and visions. It could mean that you sleep two hours less or wake up two hours earlier and create extra time for yourself. Be very mindful of "time vampires."

You can balance your time with your job. You can balance your time with your team. You can balance your time with your family. I'm very thankful for my wife and family, who understood and supported the things I was doing, which lowered the stress of handling all of these things.

I started sending connection requests like crazy. I sent over 100 connection requests a day when I first got on to LinkedIn for the first 6 to 8 months. It helped me grow as a business owner too. When I look back, I made numerous connections on LinkedIn that lacked focus on the market I was trying to reach. I was a young business owner and still learning about business. I just saw the title, registered nurse, and thought to myself that they must be the person I need to connect with, even though they didn't have access to patients struggling with the use of wearing leg bags. A quick tip when sending private messages on LinkedIn--don't make them very long.

Someone will not take the time to read a long personal message when they're just glancing through their phone, checking all the other apps. I chose to shorten my message to 3 paragraphs, and I like to add two images to provide a visual and engage the viewer. You only get a few seconds of someone's time. You have to give the message that will be enough to get them to respond. At times, I've gotten long private messages on LinkedIn, and I don't even read them. I can't. It's way too long and too much information to decipher. Less is more. It's like a 30-second elevator pitch, but this time it has to be in a direct message. If you vomit all of your information when you get someone to open your private message, then you can't expect someone to eat it. Keep it simple, allow room for a reply, and hope for the best.

The last thing I do when someone reads the message and the notification drops, I send one final sentence as my "parting shot." I would say something along the lines of, "How can I get a chance to work alongside you and help your patients struggling with the use of wearing leg bags?" Once I leave that last message, I delete the thread and keep it moving onto the next lead. I feel most comfortable with this approach because I'm not married to the outcome or their response. I also know that I've shown you everything I possibly can to help your patients. If you don't respond, then that means that you either don't have patients with leg bags or you don't care if they are struggling when wearing a leg bag. Both of those answers are okay with me because I've done my part. When I walk away from a lead, I know I've given it all I have to help their patients. I sent samples, emails, brochures, etc., and if you still don't want to do business, then I just have to keep going until I find someone who does. Once you see innovation, you are obligated to provide it to others. You can't unsee innovation.

Even though they weren't directly related to the growth of CathWear, all the connections were still beneficial. LinkedIn showed me that there was a brand new business world where I could thrive. One of the changes I made on my LinkedIn page was to add the title of an inventor to my profile. I wanted to make that the focal point of who I was so anyone that interacted with me would know it from the connection request. I knew I only had a few seconds to capture someone's attention, and with the big emphasis on nursing innovations, I wanted to match the times. I also added on my profile that I am a US Air Force Veteran. I know that America is the greatest country on earth and has the most significant military. Displaying this on my profile would break some barriers for me to reach people as they were reading my profile and assessing if they should accept the connection request. I certainly do the same thing when someone tries to contact me via social media. I strongly suggest not to "over-title" your profile page but to hone in on what you want a person researching you to know about you. For example, if you are not a keynote speaker by trade, even though you can be one, you should not add it to your profile page even though you can be.

Most people who are (international) keynote speakers find themselves to the microphone by nature. When you overwhelm your audience with all of your accolades (most people could care less about them), it is difficult for your strengths to be made visible. The profile page is not a resume for others to read. Make yourself attractive with less information to gain more visibility. You don't need to list all you've done after your name, as it presents a vast "in-your-face-look-at-who-I-am" type of person, and nobody likes a know-it-all anyway. Keep the benefits you bring to actual patient care at the forefront. That is who this is about, the patients. For example, DNP, MSF, MBA, MA, CENP, FACHE, APRN, or AGPCNP after your name is not needed, in my humble opinion. If your goal is to shove all your titles in someone's face to show what you've done, this is a great way to do that, but if your goal is to network, then maybe you can focus your approach. We have to be mindful that success can also be a deterrent to someone who lacks self-confidence. They may pass you up for another person because they think you'd never work with them or they can't afford to pay you for your part to be involved in the project. Take a look around on LinkedIn--the most influential people don't have all the titles after their name. Their value speaks for itself. We must remember to leave room for people to get to know us. It's like online dating. You meet someone who tells you their favorite color is blue, they like Chinese food and enjoy a great comedy show. On the very first date, you're wearing all blue, dinner for two at the local Chinese food spot, and tickets in hand for a comedy show to end the night. What excitement of the unknown have you left room for in that situation? Allow people to get to know you as they interact with you and uncover things about you that create value in the long run. Create a profile that tells the people you are the source they need for the journey they're on. Most of the people you're going to interact with to promote your business don't have a medical background in many circumstances. They don't even know what all of the acronyms mean, and it makes things unclear. Your vision must be simplified. If your goal is to connect, then connect at their level. Once you do that, then you can bring them high in the skies like the eagles, where it's never crowded.

We have to try to slim down to the things that matter the most and attract the people we are trying to generate partnerships with. Less is more. People will only read things that pertain to you with a very brief glance of the eye. Ask yourself: If someone was going to read about me for two seconds, what do I want them to know about me?

When I got on LinkedIn, I committed myself to not using LinkedIn as a popularity contest. I got on LinkedIn to grow CathWear. I wanted everything to be professional. I tried to move away from anything political and nothing personal or opinion-based. I didn't want to post anything faith-based either, as I could do that on my other social media pages. I just wanted to keep it solely on growing CathWear. I started posting the moments from CathWear's Facebook and Instagram pages on my LinkedIn account. I wanted to show the level of sophistication CathWear had achieved. We were a certified-veteran owned company and certified-minority owned company. I felt this was important for the audience to know who we were. Most people gravitate towards working with veterans because of our strong work ethic and such. For information on how to become veteran or minority certified, Google how to do this. Different states vary in requirements depending on location.

By this time, we had already launched on Amazon. We recently started selling CathWear units internationally as we partnered with a nurse from South Africa and sold on Amazon Canada. We also sell to patients from various countries when they visit our website. Amazon sales started to grow as we quadrupled our sales from 2019 in the first five weeks of 2020. I built a network of people who could help me get into hospitals and doctors' offices. I was speaking with nurses, physicians, and nurse practitioners all over the US, and some even across the earth, right at my fingertips. This example is why I didn't understand why someone told me that if I didn't work full time for CathWear, it was just a hobby. I spoke with nurses in other countries and built our network while pulled over on the side of the road. I was using technology to make my role as a salesperson easier. The times have changed from physically cold-calling an office when so much is accomplished with an email. Most places will not even let you past the front desk or "the gatekeeper," as I often call them. Especially now with COVID-19, you're never getting past those secretaries now. It doesn't matter if you bring 100 donuts and bagels.

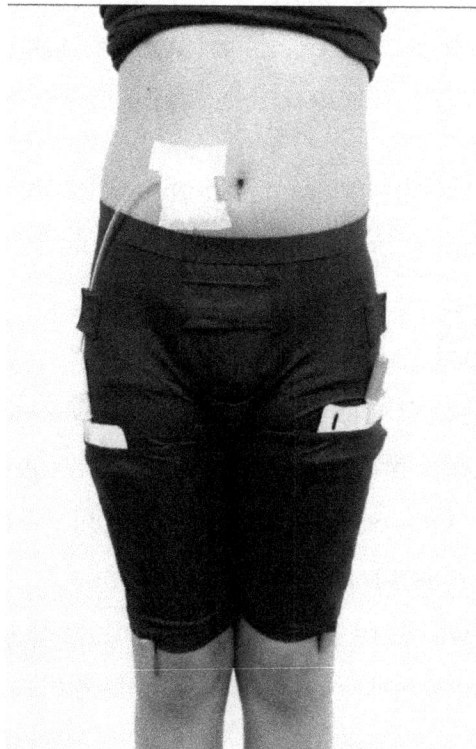

Linkedin is genuinely a virtual sales call. I highly recommend anybody that has an idea of starting a business to get on LinkedIn, find their target market, and focus all of their attention there. Once they accepted my request, I started developing the relationship by sending them a direct message. I immediately went into the message box, and I sent them a message I had saved as a cut-and-paste from a template. The message wasn't very long because I didn't want to overwhelm them with information. I realized that I needed to make my 30-second pitch into three paragraphs. I always added one or two images because I wanted to capture their attention with a visual representation of CathWear. I sent the message as soon as they accepted my request because I knew they were on the phone at that moment, and I had their attention to make my first introduction.

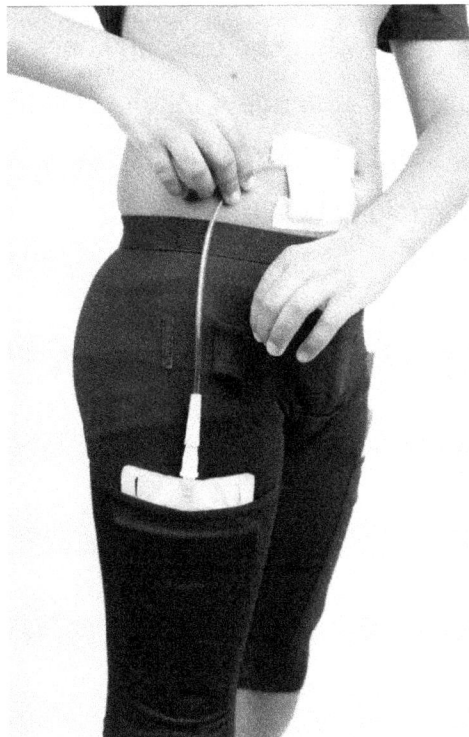

I was able to generate some leads on LinkedIn for the pediatric version of CathWear, which I had been trying to launch for over two years up to this point. We have not been able to identify the pediatric version market, and Edwin and I have not been moving in stride because of the inability to find hard data. I firmly believe Mitrofanoff drain patients and pediatric urology patients will undoubtedly benefit from our innovative design, although I know they have fewer indwelling catheters than adults. I just can't let go of this market even though we haven't been able to make any traction as of yet. I refuse to quit, and I know I will find a Urology nurse who will help me tap into this underserved patient population. We had been counseled that CathWear's original patented design is so specific with 11 claims within our utility patent that somebody could remove a feature and essentially obtain a patent. We felt very comfortable with this because removing any of the features would make a far inferior product. Someone could remove a pocket and not be infringing on our patent. When I designed the pediatric version, I modified our original design and removed one pocket from the thigh. I applied for a patent on the design to protect the adult version and protect the pediatric version. A utility patent lasts 21 years, and we are quickly approaching our halfway marker. By filing for a patent on the pediatric design, we are essentially protecting the original patent. I tried to think of a way someone would be able to "knock-off" our invention, and I filed for a design patent on it, which is the image on the cover with one pocket. I realize that we may not get approved for the patent, and this will also show me that no one else will be able to patent a modified version of CathWear.

Chapter 10: Rejection

The many connections I made didn't end up with a potential lead. It was more like 100:1. One hundred connection requests led me to one person who responded. If the situation developed further, I would send them a sample of CathWear. Generating leads was very healthy for me. In many ways, I've dealt with rejection. In some areas of my life, it set me back, but I'm older now. Not only am I more senior, but I am also hungry and eager to grow this company. Many people may not have wanted to take a chance on partnering up with a product like medical underwear, but I didn't care because I was so motivated. I spoke about this in the earlier chapters.

You can't teach somebody how to get over rejection; you can't teach somebody to send 100 connection requests a day, every day--even Saturday and Sunday. You can't teach somebody that. It has to come from within themselves. Many people's problem is that if they get rejected by a job they want or a person they like, their self-confidence becomes instantly shattered because they didn't have an abundance mindset. When you have an abundance mindset and get rejected, it's okay because you tell yourself tomorrow you will find ten more leads or meet ten new people. You know there are always possibilities. There are people less qualified that are doing the things you want to do because they decided to take action. There is a desire to be successful that has to come from within. It didn't matter when somebody rejected me or said, "NO!" Because I just knew the next person would be the person who would help me. I always felt like the subsequent connection request would be the request that would help me, and it's what fueled my fire. I was trying to find the right lead. As leads would grow cold, I started to focus my efforts on the adult urology market for suprapubic tubes for bladder cancer. We originally thought it was women who were the target gender within the market based on our research. We didn't know if it was women because they are the ones with the drain or buying the product as the natural caregiver in a family.

I started focusing my requests on the target market. The data assessed the market, and we found 30 million Americans having a catheter in place for anywhere from

2 weeks to permanently. The average person buys 1.5 pairs of underwear per year, and we sell at $40.00, giving us a market size of $1.8 Billion. 1.1 million new patients undergo a catheter procedure every year, and at $40/ unit, we can connect with a patient pool worth $66 million annually.

We grew up extremely poor, and times were indeed hard for us. We always had food and things of the sort, but money was still tight. I couldn't fathom creating a product that was too expensive and especially underwear. The team wanted to charge patients $50 per unit initially, and I couldn't do it. I tried to keep it relatively low so that all patients could have a better chance to afford our innovative design. I know what it's like to want something and not be able to afford it. I didn't want to do this to the people we were helping. What good is it to have a lovely house and a fancy car with a yacht if the people you know need it but can't afford it? Please remember this, don't pursue money, but pursue solving a problem and being a person of value. The money will take care of itself. Leaders promote their value by making themselves and what they offer available to others. Leaders keep their people in front of them and maintain the growth of the team at all times. Great leaders lead from the back of the pack. I have done numerous things within this business venture and received no monetary incentive in return. I also never asked for compensation for anything I did to help us grow CathWear. I just keep saying yes to everything asked of me, and I'll let the chips fall where they may. I believe in this philosophy, and I know that it will open more doors for me down the line where I will create revenue from my experiences of being a nurse entrepreneur.

We were even told by many others that we could charge over 100 dollars, and Medicare would cover it. This troubled me because my mother couldn't afford underwear for $50.00, let alone $100.00. We decided to price it at $39.99 per unit, and this would prove to be a great success. We then implemented a sale of 3 for $99, and this ended up being our top seller.

As CathWear developed on Amazon and our sales department grew, I started focusing my method by sending only urology surgeons. I would type in "urology practitioners," "urology chief," and "urology nurses," All different combinations of words to get our target market. I found it interesting to obtain more traction with people I didn't know and who didn't look like me than I did with people I knew and those who looked like me. I just kept pushing. What ended up happening was that I was creating awareness through LinkedIn:

- Through the posts

- Through the connection requests

- Through the messages I would send through the images I would send in people's inboxes.

Those practitioners and nurses would send their patients to our website. I would always ask patients, "Hey, how did you hear about us?" They would respond, "Well, a nurse recommended me." These referrals are how we thought it through into the business plan because we knew as patients wore CathWear to their doctor appointments, they would be like pseudo-salespeople. Not only did we have the medical professionals on LinkedIn sending us patients, but we also had the patients themselves advertising for us. It was the best-case scenario being played out right in front of our eyes.

CHAPTER 11:
INSECURITY

When I initially got LinkedIn, it was very intimidating. There is a high level of academia present on LinkedIn. I thought, "I don't have a Ph.D. or Masters. How can I speak to this person?" I needed to overcome insecurity within my mind to push forward. This also happened when I flew around the country, sitting in rooms with doctors and administrative personnel, and all the attention was on me. I remember saying to myself, "Yes, he is a doctor. Yes, this person has a Ph.D." Yet, at the same time, when it comes to CathWear, I have the 'Ph.D..' In CathWear, I'm the expert, and you are as well with your innovations and inventions. It was my job to be there. We have to be very mindful of the imposter syndrome, which can hinder personal growth and, in turn, the business's growth. As a medical professional, you have every right to be there because you are the one providing a solution to a problem that is being underserved. The more I focused on what my purpose was, growing CathWear, the more I overcame these insecurities. It wasn't about how many credentials I had behind my name. It was about marketing my product so it could get to the patients who needed it.

I posted only once a week on LinkedIn, and it was every Monday, at the same time. I posted to show the things we were doing through CathWear. I wanted to show how we were impacting patient care. I tried to gain momentum with my followers. It was engaging AND very successful. Don't let LinkedIn intimidate you. Don't let your insecurities start to manifest themselves. I was able to solidify our partnership with Byram Healthcare, a national distributor of durable medical equipment, and they are 100% script only. I sent so many connection requests to their employees on LinkedIn that it seemed as if I had reached the entire company. I contacted their marketing director and developed the lead because he saw the innovative design of my invention and how it could grow his company and help their patients. We had already obtained a partnership with Henry Schein in the previous year. They are also a national distributor. We were able to close on a distribution deal with Urocare, a distributor out of California, a distributor.

At the end of December 2020, we had been able to develop a partnership with Rudder, LLC, which is a wholesale distributor, which led us to get onto Walmart.com. Rudder was our largest distributor channel thus far, and having the opportunity to be on the Walmart website was a victory for us in so many ways. I didn't even realize we were on their website because of how hard we had all been working. Believe it or not, we were on the Walmart website for over a week, and I had no idea. That's the mindset to have. That's the way my things had changed for me. The old me would've been hanging on this opportunity every step of the way. Now we have to continue to work with Rudder and make them successful so the Walmart website can increase in traffic. Nothing is going to happen unless we work all the avenues and grow every distribution channel. It doesn't mean "distribution contract equals millions of dollars," which I thought when we started this project. It's a great start to have all of the channels, but now the hard work begins. You need to know this for your project. You need to know the work never stops but only increases in intensity as the days and weeks pass on. The visual analogy I would like to leave the reader with is the game Jenga. The more you move pieces around, the higher the risk, the easier it is to fail, and that's the best way to live: high risk, high reward. Taking these risks is where greatness comes from. Greatness never came from playing things safe. We are only here for a short amount of time. Learn to play under intense pressure--it builds character. Learn to be happy, feeling a little rushed or overwhelmed; it will bring out the best in you. It was a great feeling to see a product I invented, and we brought it to market on the Walmart website! Crazy!

We recently started working on a distribution deal with Men's Liberty, who provided a condom catheter for their client base. Edwin modified CathWear to fit their 250ml leg bag, and we were able to offer an improved quality of life for the patient wearing their product. The joint venture with Men's Liberty can be a crucial partnership because I had explained to Edwin how his modification would not work with their leg bag design, and he pushed through and went ahead with it anyway. The conversion of our design ended up working for these patients. It was better than I certainly expected. Decisions like this are why it is critical to have strong team members around you and allow people to make their own decisions within the organization's structure, and understand that not everyone thinks, talks, or acts like you. We were also able to pick up our first hospital urology clinic in Los Angeles who saw the benefits of CathWear for their suprapubic patients. Again, this is all accomplished because of our team and our desire to impact healthcare in our respected category.

It is essential to honestly assess each lead before you start to invest time and money into it. We have had some "bad leads" which were not a good fit. For example, if McDonald's wanted to purchase CathWear, we would decline the offer because people aren't looking for leg bags at a McDonald's. You have to partner up with companies who will help with your product's visibility and not just take up inventory to sit on the shelf or website. The first question I'd ask was if they sold leg bags. If they didn't, I would let them know CathWear wasn't a good fit for either of us. That was something I learned early on from Edwin. I wanted to give CathWear to everyone who would purchase it, and this was a clear indication I didn't know much about this part of owning a business. That is undoubtedly okay because I knew Edwin did, and I gained so much confidence knowing we were on the same team. Edwin is a long-range sniper when it comes to business acumen. He says he hitched his trailer to my vision. I think we both "hitched" ourselves to this vision and decided not to quit on each other despite our differences, and you can't beat a team with this type of mentality.

CathWear was also able to partner up with Uresil, who makes their gravity bag used in the interventional radiology suite post-procedure. These distribution channels took months upon months to develop. None of them were was done overnight. Through the many connections I made on LinkedIn via my relentless work ethic to growing everything I touched to its most astonishing ability, I achieved this through the many connections I made on LinkedIn.

Here are some tips I used when trying to develop a lead. They may or not work for you:

1. Find the people/competitors in your industry and contact them.

   1. If it is a competitor, then you could license your idea to them once it's protected.

2. If it is a distributor, you could get on their purchasing platform, and then their clients will know you exist.

2. I would call places and ask to speak to the nurse manager or simply ask how I could present my idea to their company.

1. I would say, "Hello, my name is Brian, and I'm a registered nurse. Can I please speak to your nurse manager?" I would say it with a clear and confident voice like I was supposed to be on that call. You can't have a shaky voice when you're making a cold call.

3. Go to their websites and see if they have a product submission page. Once you submit your idea, call their customer service number and follow up by asking who the contact person is.

4. After you find these companies, go to their LinkedIn page and try to send connection requests to everyone on their list who would be an appropriate contact point.

5. As you start developing the lead, quickly ask for the chance to send free samples or even a prototype, critical to developing a prototype.

6. I can't stress enough how vital following up on potential leads is. I would email one week and then call the following week. A very critical tip I want to share with you when sending an email is what to write within the subject line. If I had the name of a person who came from a referral, I would only put that person's name in the subject line. I wanted the recipient of the email to wonder why there was an email with the subject line having the name of someone they knew. If I simply wrote "CathWear," then the person would think it was spam because they didn't recognize the name and dismissed the email. Before I moved on from the lead, I wanted to make sure that I had done everything I could to contact them. I was comfortable being a nuisance because I knew that being a pain would either develop or close

the lead, and I was delighted with either of those happening. However, I was not comfortable with the lead being up in the air and undecided.

These are some of the methods I used to grow my inventions into sources of revenue. The techniques I have mentioned are certainly not a blueprint or a manual that will guarantee success, but like anything in life, you can take and leave what does and does not apply, and you can add your ideas along the way.

I was contacted by the American Nurses Association Advisory Innovation Board and offered a position to sit as members on their board. The opportunity was something that came to me. I didn't seek it out. I believe this to be fruit from my hard work because I didn't quit on my dreams. Hard work always pays off. I am honored to be part of such a prestigious organization, which will ultimately help me reach my goal of assisting medical professionals in overcoming any biases, statements, or paradigms that hold back inventors, innovators, and entrepreneurs worldwide. When asked if I wanted to join the ANA Advisory Innovation Board, I was interviewed on a podcast for Johnson & Johnson. I gladly accepted the interview. I remain completely blown away because who would've thought when I quit on my first invention years later that I would have an invite to be interviewed by a company with a global household name such as Johnson & Johnson?! I will now be a judge for the ANA Innovation Awards contest that they have every year. I couldn't have scripted this entrepreneur journey any better.

The goal is to impact patient care. I achieved this, and I am very thankful for LinkedIn and the people I've connected with on this platform. Every nurse who has come forward to help me, I never let it be a one-way street. I always offered myself to help them in any capacity so that they could grow within their journey. We must remember always to give back, wherever we can, and as often as we can. I have met some great people who have gone out of their way to help me get to CathWear to their patients in their respected facilities. People have called people after-hours. People have reached out to me directly without me reaching out to them initially. I am very, very thankful for those people. I have also concluded that people are reading this book who could have helped me, known they could've helped me, and for whatever reason, didn't extend the offer to help.

There's nothing I can do about their reaction or non-reaction. I recognize who these people are, and I just use it all for motivation. I respect their desire to not want alongside me and help patients together. Nursing organizations whose focus is to push nurse innovators forward, and which started in my hometown (Boston) who haven't even called me to see how they could help me grow CathWear. I was never approached and asked how I could help their organization grow with the things I've learned along my journey. I see them all over social media, talking about how they're looking to help more nurses. It puzzles me how nurses can do this to each other. As I mentioned many times throughout the book, using rejection as motivation is a skill not too many people have. It fuels my fire to see people walk right past me to move onto the next person, who may not even be as advanced along their journey as I am. However, I choose to focus on the people who have helped me. That's also a great skill, focusing on the positives and the people who show up to help you, to help more patients. If you are one of those people and you're reading this book-- thank you-- because you helped CathWear get to the right people.

CHAPTER 12:
EXIT STRATEGY

You can't celebrate your victories too long. As the saying goes, act as you belong here. CathWear, whether it's successful or not, doesn't define me. God defines me, and that's a compelling thought process to have because you don't put any emphasis on the ability of man to promote you or demote you. Nobody is in charge of your future, but you. Nobody can close the door on you, which is supposed to be open. You don't need somebody's approval to impact patient care. You will not get along with someone many times, and this does not necessarily mean there's something wrong with you or the other person, but simply that people have different business DNA, and it may not match yours. However, you will find people who have the same DNA as you, and you must be able to identify these like-minded people, gravitate towards them, learn from them, and build with them. There will always be people in life who speak about you behind your back, undermine your projects. At times they don't necessarily want to help you along your journey. It is their right not to like your social media posts, will not clap when you win or extend congratulations, and this is perfectly okay. This is life.

I want to encourage the reader of this book never to allow your skin color or background to create obstacles for you in your mind, which will then manifest in your professional life. I do not believe anyone can open or close the door on you. There's nothing that can trump an excellent work ethic and professionalism. Someone once told me, "If you were white, CathWear would've blown up by now. If you had blonde hair and blue eyes, people would be helping you at every step of this project. More leads would have come your way, and people would have been more apt to use CathWear on their patients." Someone made this comment to my wife and me during a walk in our neighborhood in the summer of 2020. For two days after I heard this comment, I lamented about the statement's validity, and it started to develop anger, resentment, and frustration in my mind. If you know me at all, you know my stance on anything focused on the color of somebody's skin. Since most of you don't know me, I will say never to allow yourself to focus on the color of somebody's skin or ethnic background, even if it is your own. After two days of pondering this statement, I verbally said that I would not allow anyone to hold the keys to my future and the impact I made in healthcare. I refused to believe that my skin color was the reason why something happened or didn't happen. I refused to have an inferiority complex placed on me by someone's projections of their feelings.

As aforementioned, I believe in an organized work ethic, and one thing that can never be beaten is somebody hungry to reach their finish line. You can't beat someone who refuses to quit. Never accept defeat and never feel as if the hands of another person destroyed you and your career. Lastly, do yourself a favor and never put a race or gender in front of a professional title. You will do a disservice to the race, gender, and the professional title simultaneously. You are not a "black nurse." You are a nurse. You are not a "black CEO." You are a CEO. You are not a "Hispanic inventor." You are an inventor. You are not a "black entrepreneur." You are an entrepreneur. You are not a "Latino engineer." You are an engineer. You are not a "male nurse." You are a nurse. You are not a "black Veteran." You are a US Veteran. When you do these things, you separate yourself from the very-thing thing you want to be involved in. We often create our barriers by blending in when we are not called to blend in; we are called to break out. The victim mentality has never been an environment for any greatness or value, but it is the environment for stagnation.

As I mentioned earlier, someone asked me where do I see myself in two years? I was going to start working with someone in a different setting, which we had met on LinkedIn. I said I saw myself selling CathWear and moving more towards public speaking. I see myself moving towards helping people grow by sharing my entrepreneurial journey and pushing this information forward. There is an enormous incentive to being transparent, and the higher you go, and the more transparent you are, you will see the paths of success illuminate themselves for you amid the darkness. All you have to do is keep your eyes on the end goal. I see myself as a keynote speaker traveling around and helping organizations develop their leaders. When I answered the question, it was very inspiring as a personal testimony to me because it let me know that I wasn't married to CathWear for the life of CathWear. I knew CathWear was just a moment in time for me, and there are greater things on the horizon that I would love to do. I love to teach. I love to push knowledge forward and uplift people. I love to share my story to inspire others and desire to impact patient care themselves. I want to inspire people not to quit on their dreams.

This is what this entrepreneurial journey is all about . . . Let It Flow!